SUPER SPORTSCARS

Clive Prew

MALLARD PRESS

Copyright © 1991 by Brompton Books Corporation

First published in the United States of America in 1991 by
The Mallard Press
Mallard Press and its accompany design and logo are trademarks of
BDD Promotional Book Company, Inc.

All rights reserved

ISBN 0-792-45597-5

Printed in Hong Kong

Page 1: The latest Porsche Carrera 911 4.

Pages 2-3: The classic lines of a Morgan Plus 4.

This page: The 1968 Corvette ushered in a new swoopy style.

CONTENTS

Introduction

1. The Power and the Glory   8
2. A Sporting Tradition   26
3. Prancing Horses & Flying Saucers 52
4. Total Driving Efficiency   76
5. Imitation and Innovation   100
Index   112

Introduction

Is it or isn't it? The argument as to exactly what constitutes a real sportscar is one of those never-ending disputes that are as old as the motor car itself. And as the years go by, so the question becomes ever more impossible to answer.

Originally, the phrase was coined to denote a car into which an Edwardian gentleman could not enter without removing his top hat. Fortunately for us all, fashions change even faster than automotive designs. Later, a sportscar meant exactly that – a car built for sporting activity. These were race and ride cars. You drove to the track, competed, then assuming you hadn't competed too enthusiastically, you drove home. Performance took precedence over appointment, and usually led to a big engine in a small, lightweight chassis. Sportscar meant two seats, an uncompromising ride, temperamental performance, get-out-and-get-under realiability, detachable soft top and side curtains. But if these alone are your benchmarks, then where do you stop?

If a sportscar must be open topped, where does that leave the Ferrari F40? If it should be spartan, where does that leave the E-type Jaguar? If it should be powerful, then where do you put the Austin Healey Sprite? Two seats? The Le Mans Bentleys were four-seaters. Competition success? How about Monte Carlo winners like the huge Jaguar Mark 7 or the diminutive Mini Cooper, and Le Mans winners like Cunningham's '53 Cadillac?

In the 1960s, the letters GT were always a good guide, but once they had been abused by every major manufacturer, adding a little borrowed glory to family sedans with mild carburetor tweaks, a body stripe and a noise muffler, they became as meaningless as the cars they graced.

While sportscars may no longer be the by-product of competition, they do tend to remain at the forefront of automotive technology. In the same way that better steels and an understand-

Above: The 1968 'Vette was a completely new departure for the company, but the curvy body was here to stay.

Left: Not the most beautiful of cars, the powerful Lotus Seven nevertheless commanded an enthusiastic following.

Right: The 1966 Ferrari 275, a fine example of a classic breed.

INTRODUCTION

ing of engine balancing promoted faster crankshaft speeds in the early days, so carbon composite materials and rear wheel steering are making cars faster today. And what developments we've seen: from front engines to rear, from transmission to transaxles, independent suspension, fiberglass, variable valve timing and almost any number of cylinders you care to mention, including the odd numbers.

But the market is changing. New models are only produced after endless analysis and market research into exactly what it is that the public wants. At one time, it was the sporting hatchback; most recently, it's been the sporting sedan. Automotive boffins can now give us big comfortable four-doors with the capacity to outdrag the sportiest of two-seaters and the handling to run rings round it. Advanced engine management has enabled us to go racing with the same engine that takes us to the shopping mall. Adjustable suspension lets us alter spring and damping rates from the drivers seat. But are these sportscars? That's another debate altogether.

Whatever the definition, one thing is for sure. Sportscars are built for the pleasure of driving. Each may exhibit its own peculiarities, but it is certain qualities, and quirks that endear each model to its owner. It's that character that helps you stand out from the crowd. Maybe that's why sportscars are presently undergoing something of a rebirth. Like nothing else, they stand up and shout your intentions. Look at me. I'm a sportscar driver.

Looking through the pages of this book, it's a sad reality that as the motor car becomes ever more sophisticated, dogged by the restraints of emission regulations, liability laws and windtunnel perfection, the days of the backyard enthusiast, fashioning a new car for public consumption are gone for ever. Our only consolation is that there are plenty good examples left to savor, and many that are yet to come.

1. The Power and the Glory

THE POWER AND THE GLORY

How strange that the country that to many is the very home of the automobile should list so few sportscars among its many thousand motoring names. Even Ford, the company that put the world on wheels, lists so few sportscars over its near 100 year history that even the enthusiast would be hard pressed to name more than a handful.

That's not to say that Americans haven't taught the world a thing or two about performance. In fact, nothing could be further from the truth. There were hot rod Model T Fords almost as soon as there were Model T Fords. And during those magical muscle car years, every US manufacturer produced cars that almost defied belief in terms of brute horsepower.

GTO, Cobra Jet, Roadrunner, Barracuda, Challenger and Charger are just a few of the names that spelt 'horsepower' to a whole generation of American youth. The Plymouth Superbird in race trim was good for 220mph and you could almost buy one over the counter. But once emission restrictions started to bite, the authorities got scared, insurance companies got positively paranoid, and the party was over. And by 1972, the muscle car was almost a thing of the past.

So where does that leave the Great American Sportscar? Well, some would say it leaves us with one, the Chevrolet Corvette. But that would be to underestimate the Great American Public.

Left: Ferrari weren't the only company to build a GTO (Gran Turismo Omologato). GTO was never really a car in its own right at Pontiac, just a package of options, albeit a very popular one, available on Tempest, Le Mans, and Catalina models. This 1971 Pontiac GTO convertible would be a rare piece today as only 661 were produced. Its 400ci engine came with 300hp at 4900rpm.

Above: The 1970 Pontiac GTO had a slightly leaner look to the front end. Just over 40,000 GTOs were built this year, including many with the 'Judge' option, – 400ci RAM AIR IV motor, with 370hp, trick wheels and tires, rear deck spoiler, black grilles, side stripes and those all-important Judge decals.

SUPER SPORTSCARS

Right: Race driver Mickey Thompson's 1969 Ford Mustang, part of a group of specially modified Mach 1 Mustangs at the Bonneville Salt Flats in September that year. The aggressive looking grille gives the car a sculptured look, barely softened by the wind-cheating headlamp covers.

Top and bottom far right: Though Ford's Mustang is regarded as one of the greatest of American muscle cars, by 1972 it was a shadow of its former self. Called a Sports Compact by Ford, it was neither sporty nor compact, thanks to an over-weight 1971 restyle and a 302ci engine with a miserable 140hp.

Although the USA has played host to more than its fair share of imports, US automotive history is littered with home-grown sports cars, developed to appeal to the guys who had brought those MGs, Healeys and Porsches back from Europe. Almost every one carries the name of its proud creator. The Devin, the Ferrer GT, the Glasspar, Maverick, Multiplex and Navajo. The Panther, Pioneer, Piranha, Ruger, Squire, Woodhill or Bangert are all among the under-financed and long forgotten list of American sportscars, most of which never got past the prototype stage. Some managed to sell a few. In fact the single-cylinder King Midget sold as many as 5000 in kit form over a 24 year period. But then again, it was billed as the world's lowest priced car; and at $270 who would argue?

Many of the best remembered also-rans were built in the '50s. The Kaiser-Darrin, built by Howard 'Dutch' Darrin between 1955 and '58 was one example, a swoopy fiberglass two-seater with a strange shell-shaped grille and even stranger sliding doors. Built from 1949-54, the Kurtis was another. Frank Kurtis, better known for his five times Indy winning chassis, built three different road cars using either Ford flathead V8 or Cadillac ohv V8s, but none were as successful as his race cars. S H 'Wacky' Arnold was another well-known character. He had Italian stylists, Bertone, rebody MG cars during 1953-54, and later built the Arnolt-Bristol with it's engine from the ex-aircraft builders. Again, neither car sold in any great quantity.

Powel Crosley Junior's 'Hot Shot' followed many previous Crosleys, like the FarmORoad utility vehicle. The Hot Shot was a tiny two-seater roadster with bug-eyed headlamps, cutaway doors and the spare wheel mounted on the trunk. They stuck to the road well and were even quite fast in a buzzy sort of way, making them great fun to drive. The later engine, the CIBA, was good for 10,000rpm, which made it very popular with the tuning firms. The later model, the 'Super Sports' was a Hot Shot with doors.

Malcolm Bricklin's claim to fame (apart from owning one of the biggest import car companies in the USA), was the Bricklin SV1. SV stood for Safety Vehicle as the car had, for example, no ashtray because smoking and driving at the same time was considered dangerous. The engine was an AMC V8, the suspension was derived from an AMC Javelin and the stylish body came with gull-wing doors and color-impregnated fiberglass bodywork. Bricklin sold 2897 cars during 1974 and '75, and even though the first 800 were said to have cost over $10,000 more to build than their sticker price, they certainly didn't lose as much money as De Lorean.

John De Lorean had an incredible track record, with major roles in creating the Pontiac GTO, Firebird and Trans Am to name but a few. He eventually became Vice-President of the GM domestic car and truck group. Yet all this success didn't stop his company crashing after only 4000 (approx) De Loreans were shipped back to the States during a mere two years of production, 1981 and 1982.

The basic design had come from Giorgio Giugiaro in '74, a stainless steel-clad plastic body with gull-wing doors, fastback roof

THE POWER AND THE GLORY

line and a Renault V6 engine and transaxle, mounted at the rear on a full length backbone chassis. They also came with a five year/50,000 mile warranty, which was a little ironic, especially for the British Government who had invested nearly 140 million dollars in the project.

Maybe De Lorean should have stayed at GM for another five years. Instead, it was GM President Elliot Estes who gave the Pontiac Fiero the go-ahead in 1978. Using parts from the GM corporate parts bin, it comprised an innovatory fully driveable space-frame chassis clothed in 'Enduraflex' plastic panels. What was originally envisaged as a high mileage 'commuter car' suddenly became GM's taut handling, fast (0-60 in around eight seconds) 'other' sportscar success story.

GM's first and foremost sportscar is, of course, the Corvette. Unlike so many of the cars in this book, the Corvette is virtually unique in automotive history. It is a car whose name has grown to overshadow even that of the company who gave it life. As Corvette has become a marque of its own, modern Corvettes don't even carry the Chevrolet name.

In the beginning, the Corvette was a sportscar in looks only. Styled for the college campus, there was no denying its beauty, but with an aging straight six, it was hardly a road burner. Even when the new Chevrolet V8 engine transformed it in '55, it was only

11

SUPER SPORTSCARS

known for straight line performance. In time though, the Corvette would grow to beat the best. And not just on the track, where it beat even Shelby's Cobra, but on the street where it belonged. This was where the Corvette legend was built, in the hands of the kids who turned Chevrolet's V8 engines into the mainstay of American performance culture.

Ever since the introduction of that first 265ci small-block Chevy engine, Corvette has always managed to prise the biggest and the fastest engines out of the GM parts bin. And once that '50s styling was consigned to history, the Corvette found its true vocation. It had the toughest most aggressive looks of any sportscar ever built. Best of all, it had the performance to match. The Europeans may have built the sleekest, sexiest, most curvaceous body shapes, but the Corvette looked like it was going to beat you even when it was standing still. And what's more, you could actually afford it.

It is literally only in the last decade that GM has repositioned its favorite sportscar to give it the European style to match its ultra-modern engineering and undeniable power and handling abilities. But it so nearly didn't happen at all. Without Ford's 1955 Thunderbird, history may have told a different story, because when GM could not shift Corvettes for love nor money, Thunderbird proved that the US public was prepared to accept a proper sportscar with open arms.

Although they may have toyed with the idea beforehand, serious Thunderbird development didn't really begin until after the Corvette was announced. By 1954, a wooden mockup was displayed at the Detroit show, and by 1955 it was not only in the dealerships, but selling like hot cakes. Marketed as a 'personal car', the Thunderbird had everything the Corvette didn't – sturdy steel bodywork, wind-up windows, a power top or lift-off hard top and a proper V8 engine.

T-bird sales beat Corvette in 1955 by almost 24:1. By 1957, a restyle brought subtle tail fins and bullet-shaped points on the bumpers, and if you took the optional Paxton-McCulloch supercharger, a more than healthy power output of up to 300hp. What a pity that Ford's commitment to four-seaters turned Thunderbird into a different car altogether for '58. As long term Corvette competitors, who knows what Ford might have turned up?

Like so many great car stories, the Corvette's has its fair share of heroes. The men whose names are not just indelibly printed in the memories of every Corvette enthusiast, but remembered by Americans with only a passing interest in automotive history. Harley Earl is one such name. As are Zora Arkus Duntov, Ed Cole and Bill Mitchell. Harley Earl, Vice-President (Design), General Motors, can be regarded as the man who fathered the Corvette. Edward Cole, who had come from Cadillac in 1952 to become Chevrolet Chief Engineer was responsible for its engine, first persuading all he could from a six-cylinder sedan unit, then finalizing the details of the new V8, lifting the cubic capacity from 231ci to 265ci and effectively saving the car from the edge of extinction.

THE POWER AND THE GLORY

Above left: The 1973 Ford Mustang was virtually the same as the '72 model; changes were restricted to a redesigned cross-hatched grille. With increasing concern over the safety of cars generally, the Mustang was now the only Ford offered as a convertible.

Above: By 1978, Mustang sales had fallen to a new low. The King Cobra Mustang was one attempt to cure the problem, though it was hardly a good looker compared with earlier models.

Right: By 1986, performance was back at Ford, with this Mustang GT.

13

SUPER SPORTSCARS

Left and below left: John De Lorean's dream car turned to a nightmare after only two years meagre production. A stainless steel-clad plastic body and Renault 2580cc V6 engine came together in a car aimed at the successful business man. But a seven year old design and gimmicks like gullwings doors did the car no favors.

Right: The Vector W2 can hardly be described as a high production sportscar, but that was never the intention of designer Gerald Wiegart. The Kevlar body hides a Chevrolet V8 engine with over 650hp.

Launched at the Waldorf Astoria ballroom in 1953, the Corvette was promoted to help reverse Chevrolet's mundane image and give GM something that would truly compete with the British sportscars that Harley Earl had driven as a college kid. The trouble was, although the public marveled at the styling and construction, many complained that the performance was as lightweight as the fiberglass body, and where were the side windows, the back seats and the affordable price? This, coupled with some off-target advertising from GM's marketing department, produced such poor sales in 1955 that the whole project was almost scrapped for good. Things were sorted out for '56, of course, when the newly restyled Corvette combined Duntov's new V8 with luxuries like wind-up windows and an optional hard top, but it was a close run thing.

Zora Arkus Duntov, a Belgian-born Russian, had already designed the famous Ardun overhead valve conversion for the side-valve Ford V8 when he gained a place at Chevrolet Research and Development. He first applied his engineering skills to the car's steering and suspension (making it 'go where it was pointed' in his own words) and then started work on the engine, managing to achieve 150.58mph at Daytona Beach in time for the 1956 launch.

It was Duntov, with Cole who later developed the fuel injection system that did so much for Corvette's racing success, bringing that all-important win at the Sebring 12 Hours in 1957, proof to the world that Corvette was a force to be reckoned with. It was also Duntov whose stamp would appear on the next stage of Corvette development, the 1963 Sting Ray, complete with bigger and better engines, and that weight-saving independent rear suspension.

THE POWER AND THE GLORY

SUPER SPORTSCARS

THE POWER AND THE GLORY

Left: Gerald Wiegart's company, Vehicle Design Force, was formed back in 1976 to build what would be the fastest sports car in the world. With total disregard for the speed limit, he achieved it with twin-turbochargers and Bosch fuel injection, a light alloy monocoque chassis and a short list of customers with plenty of spending money.

Above: Mission control. The Vector's cockpit is more like that of a fighter aircraft. But then at 186mph, you need all the information you can get.

SUPER SPORTSCARS

The Sting Ray, of course, also gave us the big-block engines - 396ci, 427ci, and even 454ci. The aluminum-headed L88 427 with 12.3:1 compression put out no less than 560bhp.

Bill Mitchell's chapter of the Corvette story virtually takes over where Earl's leaves off. As head of styling and later as Vice President of GM, he introduced the classic Sting Ray shape, derived, as it was from his own personally financed race car.

The Corvette story has not been roses all the way, of course. The 1968 model, for example, met with many a complaint. Car and Driver magazine claimed it wasn't even good enough to warrant a test. And for many, the years until 1982 marked a time when the 'Vette had lost its way. Too many customer luxuries combined with no more factory racing and little performance thanks to increasing emissions regulations. By 1980, emissions requirements and the lack of engineering know-how to overcome them, knocked California 'Vettes back to 305ci and an embarrassing 180bhp.

Thankfully, now we're into the sixth generation Corvette, things are truly back in the fast lane. An advanced uniframe chassis, trick suspension, 275/40ZR tires on 17 inch rims, six-speed manual transmission and the LT5 4-cam 32-valve V8 developed by Lotus (now owned by GM), make the latest ZR1 Corvette one of the most, if not *the* most complete sports cars on the market today. From standstill to 60mph takes around 4.2 seconds and the maximum speed is around 180mph so you certainly needn't worry about your Corvette's performance any more. And if you're worried about someone else driving your car, it even includes a lockable electronic 'valet setting', limiting the engine from a usual 380hp to only 8 inlet ports and 200hp.

With Italian good looks, shattering performance and handling to match, Corvette is once again something that GM and indeed the whole of America can be proud of. It looks like the Corvette will be listening to 'the heartbeat of America' for many years to come.

Below: 1981 Chevrolet Corvette. By now, the 'Vette was well overdue for a restyle, but spoilers and pinstripes had to do for now.

Bottom: It's the early Corvettes that stick in the memory. Although the wheels aren't standard, this '58 shows what it was all about. All Corvettes were convertible until 1963.

Right: A 1972 Corvette at Daytona Beach. By now, the muscle car era was coming to a close, power output was on the wane and the Corvette was turning to luxury motoring and little else.

Below right: By 1976 the Corvette had grown a plastic nosecone and tail section. But a catalytic converter had reduced power output to an all time low.

THE POWER AND THE GLORY

SUPER SPORTSCARS

THE POWER AND THE GLORY

Left: 1968, an all time low for Corvette. No longer treated as a special car within the GM group, Covette suffered from terrible build quality and ugly looks from the tunneled rear roof section forward. One US magazine actually claimed it was unworthy of even a test, returning the car with a list of 49 complaints after only a few days.

Previous pages: 1972 was the last year that Corvette retained its chrome bumpers. By 1972, the car was only offered with three engine options, the smallest number since 1963. Worse than that, even the LS5 454ci motor was only rated at 270hp, a far cry from the heady days of the late '60s when more than 400hp was the norm for big block options.

SUPER SPORTSCARS

Above: Whatever trials and tribulations it had suffered over the years, by 1985, Corvette was right back on track. The styling was almost Italian, the power was undoubtedly back in a big way and handling was awesome by any standards. Best of all, Corvette owners could now enjoy the thrill of 150mph soft-top motoring.

Left: On the inside, leather trim and slick high-tech LCD instrumentation set the scene.

THE POWER AND THE GLORY

Above: The LT5 badge refers to the engine in the ZR1 Corvette. On sale in Spring 1989, ZR1 was undoubtedly the greatest ever Corvette, with a six-speed manual transmission, 180mph potential, true race-car suspension and all the luxuries you'd expect for a car of this class.

Left: In the engine bay, a four-cam, 32-valve V8 with heads by F1 car designers, Lotus of England (now owned by GM). With 0-60mph in under five seconds, and the suspension to handle it, Corvette can once again hold its head high in international sportscar circles.

25

2. A Sporting Tradition

Donald Healey, Sydney Allard, Colin Chapman, Cecil Kimber, Trevor Wilkinson, William Lyons: British sportscar history lists many names. Men with a lust to go faster than the next man, but also to see their name on the front of their own sportscar. The ultimate enthusiast's dream. No other country can boast so many successful sportscar marques – some manufacturers looking to boost an otherwise stodgy image, some putting forward just the occasional sports model and others specializing in performance cars right from the start. But every one of them doing it their own way. Some, like Morgan, still build cars by hand, just as they did for their first four-wheeler back in 1935. Others, like Lotus, are always pushing back the frontiers of automotive technology whether it's in carbon composite materials, multi-valve cylinder heads or 'active' suspension.

Many a British reputation was made on the race tracks of the world. And as is so often the case in the world of motor racing, what a man lacked in finance he usually made up for in ingenuity, never afraid to use another company's components, but always adding a little magic of their own for good measure. Marcos, the alliance of Jem MARsh and Frank COStin, is an excellent case in point. Costin, combining his experience at Lister, Vanwall and Lotus with his enthusiasm for boats, built a body and chassis unit from marine plywood and covered it in fiberglass. On the face of it, the idea of a

A SPORTING TRADITION

wooden car is almost laughable. Unless you were one of the racing drivers who followed Marcos to victory in many a Formula Junior race. Later models did boast a steel chassis, incidentally, but with three liters of Ford V6 and the potential for 130mph, maybe it was just as well.

Although most independent British sportscars used engines from home manufacturers, it is the ones who looked to the USA that we remember with greatest affection. US engines in British chassis proved quite a successful formula, probably because they offered so much bang for your buck.

One of the earliest was Sydney Allard, son of a Ford dealer, who naturally chose a 221ci Ford V8 for his first production car, the K1. He followed it up with the Cadillac-powered J2X to win many a race at Watkins Glen and Pebble Beach.

Coachbuilders Richard and Alan Jensen started out with Ford V8 power too. Inspired by a request to build a car for Clark Gable on a Ford V8 chassis, they used the same engine for their first 'own label' product, but moved to Chrysler for the later CV8 and Interceptor. With four-wheel drive and Dunlop antiskid brakes, some models were regarded as the safest cars available, but moneyspinners they weren't, and financial troubles led Jensen into the hands of an American ex-Austin Healey importer, Kjell Qvale.

Left: One of the most British of sportscars, the Aston Martin DB5 replaced the DB4 in 1964, but the differences were minor. Both coupé and convertible bodies were avilable, as was an optional detachable steel hardtop. Engine capacity increased to four liters and 282hp.

Above: As the badge shows, the DB in DB5 stood for David Brown, an entrepreneur industrialist who acquired Aston Martin and Lagonda in 1947, almost as a hobby.

SUPER SPORTSCARS

Although Donald Healey's cars had fallen victim to new US safety and emission regulations by 1967, they certainly left their mark. Healey was already in his 50s when the Austin A90-based Austin-Healey 100/4 came to fruition. The six-cylinder 100/6 version and its bigger brother the famous Healey 3000 have always been well respected in sportscar circles.

It would be a mistake to forget the Austin Healey Sprite. Despite its frog-eyed appearance, tiny 948cc engine and low 43bhp power output, the Sprite was always a well-loved little roadster and with its wind-in-the-hair style, nippy handling and unmistakable character, nobody could deny it wasn't a real sportscar.

With the demise of his own company, Healey, by now in his 70s, joined up with Jensen and Qvale to launch the Jensen-Healey in 1972. But teething troubles with the new Lotus twin-cam engine (it hadn't even appeared in a Lotus at that time) and rust problems with the body didn't help sales at all. Its successor, the Jensen GT (Healey had withdrawn by then) fared just as badly, and by 1976 they were both history.

The most famous US/British partnerships all appear to have the Carroll Shelby name attached to them in one way or another. The best-known must be the AC Cobra, unless you're American, of course, where it was known as the Shelby Cobra.

Shelby's original idea was to squeeze the new small-block Ford V8 into the nimble AC Ace rolling chassis. The Ace, which first appeared at the Motor Show in 1953, had used a variety of engines previously so AC were more than happy to oblige. Engineless chassis/bodyshell units were shipped to Venice, California and Shelby did the rest. First the 260ci motor, then the 289ci, then the infamous 427ci big block Cobras all made their reputations on the

Above right: The latest in a prestigious line, the Aston Martin Virage, here in coupé form. When first announced, the new Virage was in such demand that most customers placed huge deposits without even seeing a car.

Right: The Aston Martin Zagato is a highly prized item. Bodied by Zagato in Milan, Italy, only 19 were ever built.

Far right: The Virage engine was the latest in the line of Aston Martin V8s. Its light alloy construction and 5.3 liter capacity ensure all the power you need.

A SPORTING TRADITION

29

SUPER SPORTSCARS

race tracks of the world, and the heavier, slower, but infinitely more driveable 428ci version made its mark on the street.

Nowadays, the Cobra banner is held by a small company called Autocraft, working in the shadow of the famous Brooklands racing circuit. Though, as they have just promised the next five years production to Japan, the chances of securing one of their Mk 4 Cobras is somewhat slight. Rumors also abound that Shelby himself is intending to build a few more Cobras in the near future, so stand by your cheque books.

Shelby's other involvement in British sportscars is every bit as exciting. Firstly, there is the Ford GT40. While Shelby's Cobras were obviously Ford powered, they weren't Fords. Ford wanted their own trophies, not Shelby's. The car to do it was the Ford GT40, and the race to do it was the Le Mans 24hrs, a goal they fully achieved in 1966 with a 1-2-3 procession. The irony was that, in the end, the first American car to win Le Mans needed Shelby's involvement, as team director, to make it happen.

So fast was the GT40 that in 1967 the FIA changed the rules to limit 'prototypes' to three liters, but 'production sportscars' were allowed five liters, which was why later racers used a 289ci V8 engine. It was this engine that powered the Mk3 GT40 that Shelby American offered in 1967 in roadgoing trim. Though at a base of $18,500, it was three times the price of a fully loaded '67 Corvette. Then again, the Corvette hadn't won Le Mans.

The final chapter of the Shelby story involves the Sunbeam Alpine from Britain's Rootes Group. Like many a British sportscar, the early Alpine was more sporting in looks than in spirit. It did improve, building to 1725cc and 92hp in 1965, but when you consider that the 1965 Corvette had 365hp, it was obviously in need of some muscle.

Under Shelby's direction, a 260ci Ford V8 was shoehorned into the tiny engine bay by Jensen, and the Sunbeam Tiger was born. At 164hp it was hardly a Corvette, but it was still twice as powerful as the four-cylinder version and it cut the Alpine's 0-60mph time in half. Unfortunately, the Rootes Group were bought by Chrysler just as the Tiger was being launched. So despite a later 289ci, 200hp version, Chrysler just couldn't accept that Ford engine any longer, and by 1967 the fun was over.

Echoing the AC story is that of TVR, founded back in 1954 by Trevor Wilkinson and Bernard Williams. Jack Griffiths, a New York race car garage owner, asked TVR to supply engineless TVR Granturas so he could also fit small-block Fords over in theStates. The TVR Griffith was supposedly good for 155mph with handling to match, but unlike AC's, TVR's project was dogged by bad luck and the company closed in 1965, only to be revived two years later in a relaunch that has taken the company from strength to strength, peaking with a new model for 1991 once again called the TVR Griffith.

Colin Chapman was one of those creative designers who urged others around him' to find solutions, look for new goals, assess problems and calculate the most logical, and correct solution. In the beginning, Lotus cars were functional driving machines. Beautiful objects of automotive desire they weren't, but winners on the track and high performers on the road, they definitely were. It was Chapman's constant willingness to try something new, plus his obsession for lightweight construction, that led to his first roadgoing GT, the Mk 14 or Lotus Elite of 1957 and the first car with unitized fiberglass construction.

Above: Announced in 1990, the latest Aston Martin is the Virage Volante, continuing their great tradition in convertible motoring.

Right: The Aston Martin DB4 Zagato, one of the most desirable and to many the most beautiful of all Aston Martins.

30

SUPER SPORTSCARS

Left: The Daimler SP250, or 'Dart' as it was known in England, used the chassis from a Triumph TR3A, a fiberglass body and a 2.5 liter 'Hemi' engine. Sales were never good though and production was ended after just 2700 units.

Below: The Marcos originally went down in history as one of the few sports cars ever built with a wooden chassis. This 1969 version was the first with the later tubular steel spaceframe.

This was no Corvette — a glass body on a steel chassis — but a lightweight fiberglass platform for an all-aluminum four-cylinder engine from Coventry Climax. Unfortunately this might have been a good idea, but it wasn't a good design and early chassis failures soon spelt disaster. The only other cars to use the same concept were the Rochdale Olympic and the Hillman Imp-based Clan Crusader, built by ex-Lotus development engineer, Paul Haussauer. Needless to say, both went the same way as the Elite, but fortunately for Lotus, they had the beautiful Elan by 1961, plus, of course, the legendary Lotus Seven.

Debuted alongside the Elite in 1957, the Lotus Seven was almost an engine on wheels. And what it lacked in the way of bodywork or creature comforts, it more than made up for with ferocious acceleration and race track roadholding. Eventually the rights to the Seven were sold to Caterham Cars, a small independent concern who still builds them today with Vauxhall 2.0-liter 16-valve engines and at least 150 bhp.

Lotus's Elan and later Elan +2 were neat little cars with stylish bodies and an engine that matched a Ford block with a Lotus-designed twin-cam head. Always in the vanguard of sports and race car development, the Elan's sheet steel backbone chassis, with its soft springs and firm damping, really handled well. Like many an early Lotus, it was offered in kit form too, which not only saved the builder the cost of factory assembly, but also managed to circumvent the British sales tax on new cars. The mid-engined Europa came next (with first a Renault then a Ford/Lotus engine) followed by a string of equally exciting cars, including another Elite and the Excel.

A SPORTING TRADITION

Nowadays, as part of General Motors, Lotus are almost too busy developing cars for other makers, like the 180mph twin-turbo Carlton, a four-door Q-car from Britain's family car builders, Vauxhall. But their own line-up is still as exciting as ever, comprising the new Elan, the Excel, the Esprit and awesome Esprit Turbo, with Garrett T3 turbocharged engine and roadholding (especially in SE trim) that can only come from a company at the very peak of Formula 1 for so many years.

While Lotus's first cars were built for the race track, Cecil Kimber's were purely in the line of new coachwork for another company's chassis. And from the simplest beginnings, Morris Garages (MG) grew to build what are still regarded as the quintessential English sportscar by many enthusiasts on both sides of the Atlantic.

The T-series MGs beginning in 1936 and taking in the TC, TD, TF, and TF1500 were the first of the line, closely followed by the MGA with its smooth lines and peppy, if not superquick engines. The twin-cam version boasted 100hp. Next in line, the MGB, MGB GT and MGB GT V8 were less attractive than the MGA, but at least they had wind-up windows. Although they lasted until 1980, bigger US-regulation bumpers did them no favors, nor did emission controls, but they still managed to sell in vast numbers. The USA didn't get the 3.5 liter aluminum V8 version, which was a pity, because it showed a decent turn of speed. This is more than can be said for the abortive MGC, an MGB with an Austin 3-liter straight six. The longest lasting MG was the Midget. Basically a Mk 2 Austin Healey Sprite in all but badging, it was offered from 1961 to as late as '79 when the historic Abingdon plant closed forever.

Throughout the MG years, its closest competitor was Triumph, whose sportscars began with the TR2 in 1953, and moved up through TR3, TR4, TR5, TR6, the wedge-shaped TR7 and even a TR8, which was a TR7 with Rover's 3.5 liter V8, the engine it was supposed to have in the first place. Other Triumphs included the Spitfire and GT6. Styled by Michelotti and based on a new backbone chassis with swing-axle rear suspension (which endowed it with somewhat 'interesting' handling), the Spitfire sold in huge quantities, lasting until the Mk 4 with 1500cc, a redesigned rear axle and raised bumpers to match US regulations. The GT6, a coupé-backed 2-liter six-cylinder version lasted until 1973.

If Ferrari spells Italian sportscar, then Jaguar spells British. Yet, while Ferrari built so many different cars with different styling and many a new motor, the Jaguar story is almost the tale of just one engine. William Lyons had built cars before the famous Jaguars,

SUPER SPORTSCARS

Right: Triumph is a sports car name that goes right back to the 1920s. The TR6 model was a revise of an original Michelotti design by Karmann of Germany, taking a break from convertible Volkswagens. These are a 1968 model on the left and a 1974 version on the right.

Below: The later TR8 was the last of the TR series, equipped with a Buick-derived 3.5 liter V8. This one has been modified for rally practice.

34

A SPORTING TRADITION

first as Swallow, and later as SS Cars, but SS wasn't an ideal name so soon after the war. Jaguar became the new name and XK120 became the product, so named because it was repeatedly good for 120mph.

The new six-cylinder engine commanded more work than the rest of the car put together, even including the technical advancements of torsion bar front suspension. Almost old fashioned in its approach, the in-line six used twin overhead camshafts, a long stroke with a main bearing between each two crank throws, and hemispherical cylinder heads with inclined valves. It was good for 160hp and up to 6000rpm from its 3.5 liters, but it wasn't without its faults, either. The vast cast iron block got very hot for a start, and the oil would push past the valve guides into the combustion chambers actually draining the sump on a long run. But by 1949, Jaguar's racing activity had proved its worth and the engine reached new levels of refinement. That it is still used by Jaguar today, albeit in slightly altered format, says it all.

Below: Still building sports cars by hand, Morgan are one of Britain's few remaining independent car manufacturers. This is a 1972 Morgan 4/4.

Right: A short involvement between Donald Healey and coach-builders, Jensen led to the Jensen Healey. Lotus provided the 140hp engines.

35

SUPER SPORTSCARS

A SPORTING TRADITION

Left: When Carroll Shelby got his hands on John Tojeiro's AC Ace, the result was the Ford 289ci AC Cobra, one of the most revered sports cars ever built. Built in various forms over its six year history, the car never produced less than 260hp. Not bad for a car that weighed in at around 2000 pounds.

Above: After many take-overs and buyouts, the AC ME 3000 was one of the last modern cars to bear the AC name. Few were produced.

Even though it was never intended for quantity production, demand for the XK120 was massive, mainly because, like so many of the Jaguars that followed, it was such good value for money. All of a sudden, stylish, svelte sports cars were no longer the preserve of the rich, nor even the skilful driver. Helped by the racing success of the XK-based C and D type Le Mans winners, sales remained high. XK140 followed with tougher styling and 190bhp. Then XK150, far more civilized than its predecessors, with good lines, disc brakes and even wind-up windows. Power and capacity went up to 3.8 liters and 220hp (or 265bhp in XK150S spec) and the XK150 became the biggest seller of them all. As usual though, something better was round the corner, the XKE, or E-type.

Low, curvy, sexy, even phallic, the E-type was the car that everyone wanted. Not just the traditional sports car types, but pop stars and actresses. The rich formed an orderly queue, and the rest had something new to aspire to. Styled in-house by Malcolm Sayer, the car used a monocoque bodyshell with a tube frame front clip, and a tilting hood/front fender/nose section just like a race car. The price was outrageously cheap too, for a car with the potential for 150mph. With the exception of the longer 2+2 version and a move to 4.2 liters in 1965, the six-cylinder XKE lasted more or less unchanged for ten years until 1971. But again, something better was on the cards.

SUPER SPORTSCARS

The Series III V12 XKE was yet another sensational Jaguar. The 5.3 liter all-aluminum, 60-degree V12 had a single cam per bank, and combustion chambers in the pistons rather than the head to give it 272bhp. Suddenly, here was a Jaguar to compete with the likes of Ferrari and Lamborghini. To accommodate the massive engine, they used the longer 2+2 chassis, making the roadster body look even longer and more cigar-like. Unfortunately, though, it was also looking a bit dated by now and until the later XJS finally lost its roof, the world had to go without a convertible Jaguar for several years. We're still waiting for a new sporting Jaguar, of course, but if Ford (Jaguar's new owners) keep their promise, the XJ220 limited production, highly priced supercar, should be well worth the wait.

Aston Martin didn't get into the sportscar business until wealthy industrialist David Brown bought the company in 1947. And even then his influence wasn't really felt until the DB2. Sleeker and lower than the DB1 and equipped with a powerful 2.6 liter twin-cam Lagonda engine (David Brown had bought Lagonda too), it wasn't the cheapest of sportscars but, well received, it set the scene for the future.

Next came the DB2/4 (four seats) then the DB Mark III (third version of the DB2), faster, more secure and better looking than ever. Yet the all-new DB4 of 1958, assembled at the new Newport Pagnell facility, was better still. Built on Superlegerra (super light) principles, the bodies were built by Touring and comprised aluminum panels over a lattice of small tubes, helping it to 140mph or more in the race-bred GT and Zagato versions.

The DB5, known to millions simply as 'the James Bond car', was basically a rebodied DB4. But a bigger engine, more power, and both Volante (convertible) and Vantage (325hp) options all made a difference. The DB6 merely stretched the wheelbase, added a new rear end treatment and spelt the end of Superleggera techniques. The DBS, styled by William Towns (who had gone to Aston just to design seats!), brought the first Aston with a four-headlamp grille, and finally added that much needed De Dion rear axle.

The final chapter introduces the Aston Martin V8 engine, 5.3 liters of pure muscle, light alloy construction and twin-camshafts per bank. Introduced first for racing, this beautiful piece of automotive engineering has powered every Aston Martin since 1969, from the first DBS V8, through AM V8, right up to the very latest Virage and Virage Volante. Under the able guidance of Victor Gauntlett, Aston Martin's future has never looked rosier than today, building cars of the highest quality in both engineering and finish. And building them very much in the best English tradition – by hand.

Right: The AC Mk4, built on the site of the old Brooklands racing circuit, continues the Cobra tradition with hand-made cars many built on the same jigs as the original.

A SPORTING TRADITION

39

SUPER SPORTSCARS

A SPORTING TRADITION

Left and below: Although it began as a Ford-only project, it took Caroll Shelby's involvement to gain the all-important 1-2-3 at Le Mans in 1966. GT40s came with either 289ci or the monstrous 427ci motor, which helped it to speeds of 250mph at Le Mans. Very few were ever made, and it is now highly-prized by collectors.

Right: The interior of this 1965 Mk I is fairly spartan, as befits such a serious racing car. Few concessions were made when it was converted to road-going form.

41

SUPER SPORTSCARS

Right: The power behind the new Lotus Elan. Just one of the benefits of being bought by General Motors was access to their parts bin. This 16v twin-cam turbo-charged 1600cc unit comes from Isuzu.

A SPORTING TRADITION

Above: The new Lotus Elan SE may look totally different to its early counterpart, but it's not too far away in spirit. The glass-fiber bodyshell is retained, as is the wind-in-the-hair stance. Good for almost 140mph and 0-60mph in under six seconds, it certainly retains the Lotus spirit too.

Left: Introduced in 1962, the original Elan was Colin Chapman's first really practical road car. Pretty, quick and agile, it came with a sheet steel backbone chassis, split at each end like a tuning fork, all independent suspension and the potential for almost 120mph.

SUPER SPORTSCARS

Right: A roller skate with an engine at the front. The Lotus Seven was never the most luxurious sports car in the world, but it was certainly one of the most exciting.

Above: At the heart of the Lotus Seven, the legendary twin-cam engine. Ford-based with Lotus head and twin Weber carburetors it endowed the super-lightweight car with shattering performance.

44

A SPORTING TRADITION

Below: When Formula 1 experience is applied to road-car design, the result is a car like the Lotus Esprit Turbo. This wedge-shaped projectile with its race-car underpinnings and all-alloy 2.2-liter motor pushed maximum speed to 150mph and earned superstar status in the hands of James Bond in the film *The Spy Who Loved Me.*

Above: Bug eyes and spindly suspension. Good looks were never the Lotus Seven's strong point, but what it lacked in show, it certainly made up for in go.

45

SUPER SPORTSCARS

Right: The TVR Griffith was built in Britain, shipped to the United States minus engine, fitted with 289ci small-block Ford V8 then shipped back to England. Needless to say, performance was shattering.

Far right: The TVR Tasmin moved up from V6 to Rover V8 power for this 350i version, available in both hard and soft top.

Below right; One of the marque's most attractive cars, the swoopy-looking MGA waved goodbye in 1962.

Below: The TVR 420 SEAC took the all-alloy Rover V8 out to 4.2 liters, with even more power at around 300hp and the potential for over 150mph.

46

A SPORTING TRADITION

47

SUPER SPORTSCARS

Left: The legendary E-type or XKE Jaguar sprang from the D-type race car, which had won Le Mans. In 1957, a few D-types were sold in road-going trim as the XK-SS, an immensely fast and desirable Jaguar.

Right: The XJS Cabriolet. This 1983 version shows how Jaguar retained the roll bar and window frames for many years before moving to a full electrically operated soft-top.

Below: Surely the sleekest of all cats, the E-type Jaguar, seen here in very early form with small side hood catches. Purists will note that the headlamp buckets should be silver.

48

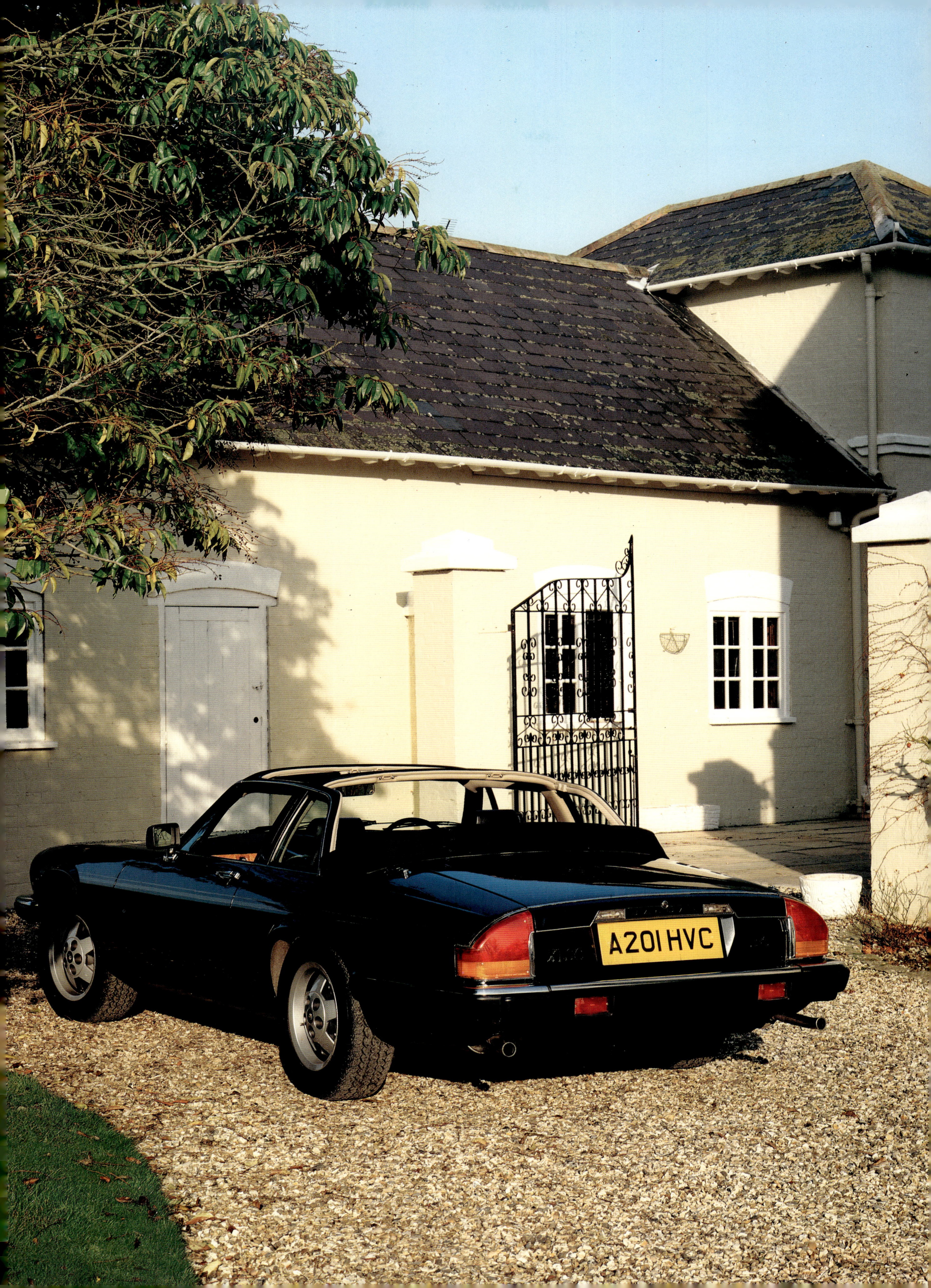
A201 HVC

SUPER SPORTSCARS

Left: Tires don't come much lower than these 295/40 ZR17s, on the front of the Jaguar XJ220.

Right: Styled by Keith Halfet and Jaguar design head, Geoff Lawson, the XJ220 started life as a design exercise, but public reaction was so great that deposits were taken and lucky customers are waiting for their Jaguar supercars.

Left: You pay your money and you take your seat. In this case, a leather-trimmed seat, just high enough to see what's coming at you at 200mph.

Right: Looking good from any angle, the XJ220 is just awesome in the power department. The prototype came with a twin-cam version of the Jaguar V12 engine, but a street version of Jaguar Sport's turbo-charged 3.5 liter racing engine is slated for series production.

50

A SPORTING TRADITION

3. Prancing Horses & Flying Saucers

PRANCING HORSES & FLYING SAUCERS

To say that the Italians love their sportscars, would be to state the obvious. In Italy, every driver is a would-be racing driver, and driving with *brio* (verve) is not only acceptable, but positively encouraged. It is the great Italian marques that evoke pictures and memories of everything a true sportscar should be. And so they should, for the true Italian sportscar not only reflects the nation's fiery temperament, but its love for all things stylish.

The names of the great Italian marques carry such weight that individual models hardly matter. It is enough that a Ferrari is a Ferrari and any car bearing the Prancing Horse emblem is worthy enough. In the same way, a car styled by Ghia, Bertone, PininFarina or Ital Design will always carry that certain something extra, not to mention a guarantee of acceptability.

With so much Italian sportscar activity concentrated in such a small area in the north of the country, it is hardly surprising that the histories of so many of the great names are intertwined. Giorgio Giugiaro, for example, worked at both Bertone and Ghia before starting Ital Design. Ghia, along with Maserati were bought and sold by De Tomaso. And Enzo Ferrari was refused a job at Fiat before he started at Alfa Romeo. Later, both Ferrari and Alfa, along with Lancia, would be owned by Fiat, of course.

Alfa Romeo's greatest days came before the Second World War when the great P1, P2 and P3 Grand Prix cars swept all before them, coaxed to victory by Mussolini's orders to Race and Win for Italy; later Enzo Ferrari ran the Alfa race team between 1933 and 1938. After the war, it was the 6C 2500 that put their name back on a roadgoing sportscar. It may have been a little on the large side for true sportscar status, but the 1900 and the very rare (nine were built) 'Disco Volante' (Flying Saucer), certainly made up for it.

Built to run alongside the 1900, the Giulietta of 1954-63 was a tiny car, first a sedan and then a two-seater spyder. Equipped with an equally tiny 1.3-liter twin-cam engine, the Giulietta was quite a fast car, and even faster when power was upped to 90hp in the Veloce model. Later and bigger versions, the Alfa Romeo 2000 and 2600 continued the spyder style with their Carrozzeria Touring bodies, but they were pricey and never quite as much fun as the little Giulietta.

The next Alfa Spyder was announced in 1966, originally called the Duetto. Designed by PininFarina, it has now been the shape of Alfa Romeo roadsters for well over 20 years, though they did chop its tail off in 1971 and swap the 1600 for first a 1750 and then a 2-liter engine.

There is one other Alfa to note, however. The Montreal was originally only intended as a one-off to represent the Italian motor industry at the Expo '67 in Montreal, Canada. But in 1972, it reached production and sales should really have taken off as rapidly as the car itself. But the 3-liter, four-cam aluminum V8, all wrapped up in a swoopy Bertone-designed shell sold badly due to lack of promotion and lasted only three years.

Left: They don't come more Italian than Ferrari. This is the Dino 246GT, one of the marque's biggest successes in sales terms.

Overleaf: Like many of the later Ferrari Spyders, the 308 GTS was more of a Targo than a real convertible. This is a US-spec Quattrovalvole.

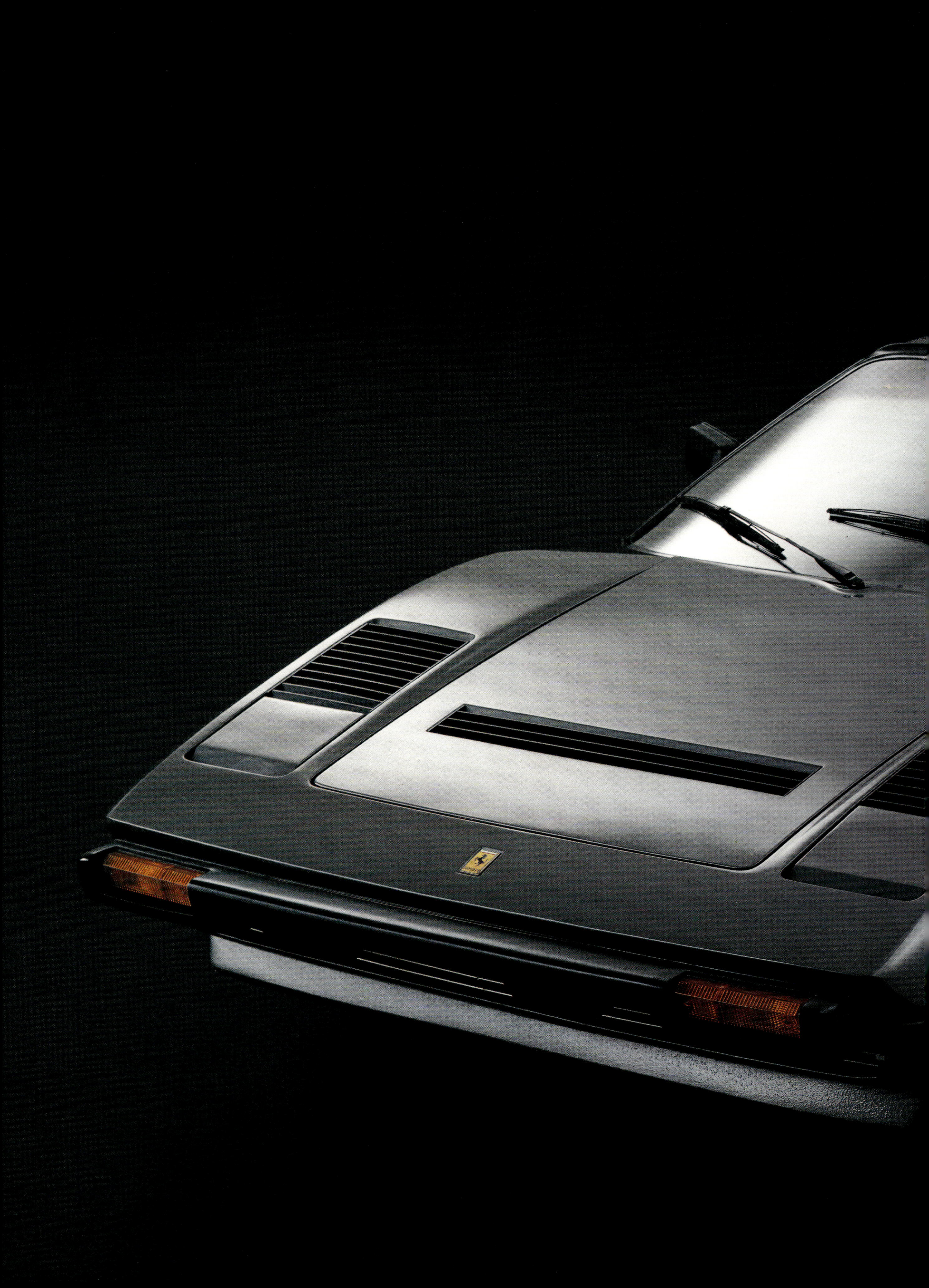

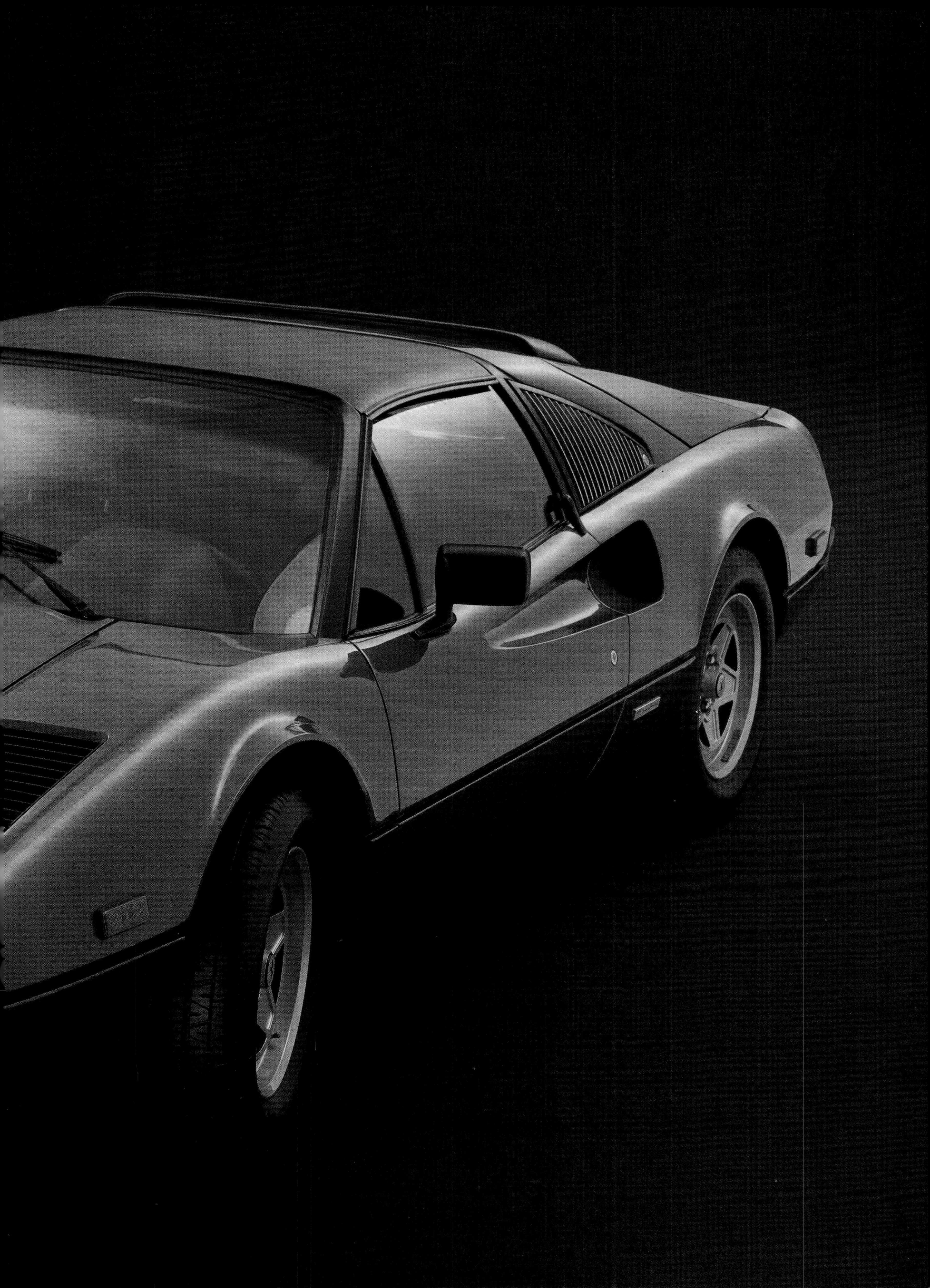

SUPER SPORTSCARS

58

PRANCING HORSES & FLYING SAUCERS

Left: Successor to the much-admired 512BB, the Ferrari Testarossa was powered by the same four-cam flat-12 type engine. But the massive width of the car (78 inches), plus those futuristic side fins gave it a style of its own.

Right: Continuing the fins, the latest Ferrari, the 348tb uses a 32-valve V8. The waiting list is so long, that Ferrari have stopped taking orders.

Below: The ultimate supercar? Well, for now at least, it's certainly the ultimate Ferrari. The F40 speaks for itself.

SUPER SPORTSCARS

Present day owners of Ferrari, Fiat have built sportscars for almost as long as there have been cars. Even the 1904 Fiat 24hp was available in sports trim. And in 1922, a Fiat won the French Grand Prix almost an hour ahead of the only other car to finish, a Bugatti. So complete was their domination of the sport that all of the other famous names of the day stayed away, knowing they were hopelessly outclassed. We have to move to 1959 to find their first volume-production roadgoing sportscar. When PininFarina was called upon to remodel the best-selling, but boring 1200 sedan, the ugly duckling was turned into a swan in the shape of the 1200 Spyder. Fiat supplied the floorpans and PininFarina built, painted and trimmed the bodies. Launched at the same time as the 1200 was a 1500, with an OSCA-built twin-cam engine. The 1500 later became 1500S which then became 1600S before they gave way to the Fiat 124, another Fiat spyder dynasty that lasted right through to 1985.

The 124 formula was one that remained almost untouched for 15 years, though engines ranged from the original 1438cc 96bhp unit through a 1600, a 1750, a 2-liter, a turbo-charged 2-liter (USA only) and a supercharged version (Europe only). But sales dwindled to such a low by 1985 that PininFarina finally called it a day.

Part of the reason for its demise was undoubtedly the Fiat X1/9, announced in 1972. Small, nippy and superbly forgiving in the handling department, X1/9 was the quintessential Italian sportscar. Using many Fiat 128 parts, it started life as a somewhat sluggish 1.3 liter, but later substitution of the newer Strada engine at 1498cc helped, as did a five speed transmission and Bosch fuel injection. With its all-independent MacPherson strut suspension, it certainly stuck to the road, even it you did feel like a sardine driving it.

Vincenzo Lancia worked for Fiat from an early age, starting his own company in November 1906, but like Fiat, he never really concentrated on production sportscars until much later on. Cars like the B24GT of 1957 with cabriolet bodywork by PininFarina and the Flaminia Sport by Zagato all held the Lancia banner in the sportscar market. As part of the Fiat empire from 1969, it is not surprising that many of their later cars were powered by Fiat products. The Lancia Beta Monte Carlo was actually going to be a Fiat when it was first conceived. Coded the X1/20 by PininFarina to follow on from the X1/9, it even sported a 1995cc version of the Fiat twin-cam, mounted transversely behind the driver. Revealed at the 1975 Geneva show, the new Lancia was named Monte Carlo to commemorate them winning the rally of the same name with their recently homologated rally contender, the Stratos. In the USA, however, the name was changed to Scorpion because GM had already claimed Monte Carlo for themselves.

The Stratos was only produced for two short years as a homologation special – a rally car for the road. With its 190hp Ferrari Dino 246GT engine, it won the World Rally Championship three years running from 1974-76 and even managed to win the Monte Carlo rally as late as 1979.

The Maserati brothers had already left the company that bore their name by the time their first road car hit the streets. Three of six, Alfieri, Bindo and Ernesto set up Officina Alfieri Maserati in 1914, adopting the traditional trident symbol of Bologna as their badge. When Alfieri died in 1932 they were joined by the fourth brother Ettore, but the company was soon sold to the Orsi family from Modena. Once their contracts ran out in 1947 the Maseratis did set up on their own once again, but under the new name of OSCA.

60

PRANCING HORSES & FLYING SAUCERS

Right and below; A beautiful Lamborghini Countach. With a massive V12 engine and race-tired suspension, it was always a super car, but with these distinctive good looks, performance is almost irrelevant.

SUPER SPORTSCARS

PRANCING HORSES & FLYING SAUCERS

Left: In profile, has there ever been a more dramatic car? This is a no-compromise sports car. There's very little room for luggage, very little chance to see where you've been, and definitely no room for children.

Below left: How do you follow the Countach? Well, here it is. The Lamborghini Diablo, again designed by Marcello Gandini is different, but many would say, no better.

Below: Whichever way you view it, the impact is the same. And everywhere you look, a surprise. The windscreen wiper looks like it would be more at home on the front of a train.

63

SUPER SPORTSCARS

Right: The 1973 Alfa Romeo Montreal was designed for the 1967 World Expo in Canada, yet surfaced in full production some five years later with a 3-liter four-cam light alloy V8 and body by Bertone.

Far right: The Alfa Romeo Spyder has lasted for many years in many guises. This is a 2.0 liter Veloce Spyder from 1976.

Below right: The Lancia Stratos lasted only two years, but in its short life managed to win the World Rally Championship three years running from 1974-6.

That first Maserati road car, the A6/1500 with coachwork by PininFarina was designed by Ernesto Maserati just before the war, but didn't actually see the light of day until 1946. Although it was hardly the fastest car on the road, 61 were produced and the chassis provided an excellent base for its successors, the stylish and very desirable A6G and A6G/2000. Both of these came with six-cylinder engines, the latter ending up with a detuned version of their twin-cam Formula 2 engine.

The next in line, coming in 1957, was the first in what would prove a long run of excellent sportscars. The 3500 series, launched at the Geneva Show in 1957, were high performance luxury road cars very much in the Ferrari mould. They came with a twin-cam, six-cylinder engine, of just under its 3.5-liter designation (though a few, called the 5000GT, came with a big twin-cam V8), four wheel discs, and either a coupé body by Touring of Milan or a convertible by Vignale of Turin.

Much like Ferrari, the full list of Maserati models takes in a wide and varied assortment, including the 4-liter Sebring and Mistrale, the Mexico, the beautiful Ghibli, created by a young Giorgio Giugiaro with the 330hp 4.7-liter four-cam V8, and its replacement, the Khamsin.

In the mid-'60s, Maserati was taken over for a second time, this time by Citroën, who provided the development money for a new mid-engined car, the Bora. One of the first projects for Ital Design, newly formed under Giorgio Giugiaro, the Bora and its V6-engined partner, the Merak, became the first mid-engined Maseratis. The Bora took the twin-cam 4.7-liter V8 with 310hp, soon upgraded to 4.9 liters. The V6 Merak carried nowhere near the horsepower (182bhp in USA spec) but with virtually the same chassis and running gear was still an excellent car and outlived Bora by three years.

PRANCING HORSES & FLYING SAUCERS

All of which brings us to Alejandro De Tomaso, an Argentinian, who emigrated to Italy via the USA, and took control of Maserati in 1976 after Citroën had cast them adrift. A late entrant to the sports-car market, De Tomaso's first real road car was the 1.5-liter Vellalunga in 1964, followed by the Mancusta (mongoose) in 1967. With its 289GT Ford V8 engine, its main characteristic was too much torque for the backbone chassis, so handling was pot-luck to say the least.

Not one to let the grass grow under his feet, De Tomaso had made further automotive acquisitions by now, including Ghia, the styling company, and it was them, or to be more exact, employee Tom Tjaarda, who designed their best known supercar. De Tomaso proposed that the incredible Pantera, with its pressed steel chassis, 351ci Ford V8 and beautiful yet tough-looking body, be marketed by Ford as a showroom image builder. And true to form the Pantera proved far more popular in the USA, where there was much less resistance to its 'Yankee' engine.

The Lamborghini connection began right at the marque's birth. Ferruccio Lamborghini, after owning many a Ferrari, finally decided that he could improve on the breed, but needed an engine for this first car. Bizzarrini designed him the quad-cam V12 that found its way into the 350GT, and 400GT. Their replacement, the Islero, used the same engine, but was always overshadowed by its room mates, the four-seater Espada and the stunning Miura.

SUPER SPORTSCARS

PRANCING HORSES & FLYING SAUCERS

Left: The Lancia Beta Monte Carlo was going to be a Fiat, but actually ended up at the Geneva Show in 1975 with a Lancia badge. In the USA it was called Scorpion because GM already owned the Monte Carlo name.

Far left: The latest in the Lancia hot hatch range, a Delta Integrale 16-valve. This one is a right-hand-drive conversion.

Above: Not many cars have ever boasted a trunk at both ends, but the Fiat X1/9 did. Lasting over 16 years, the X1/9 was the tiny car with a big sporting spirit. The transversely mounted engine sat behind the driver giving it excellent weight bias and road manners.

Left: Lancia Stratos in full rally livery. Powered by the 190hp Ferrari V6, the street version was good for 0-60mph in six seconds, so what the rally car could with a good 300hp is anybody's guess. Suffice to say, it was enough to win the Monte Carlo rally in 1979, even three years after it was retired by the works team.

67

SUPER SPORTSCARS

PRANCING HORSES & FLYING SAUCERS

Regarded by many as the most beautiful car of them all (styled by Marcello Gandini at Bertone), the Miura was also radically engineered with its V12, transversely-mounted in the rear. Launched in 1966 at Geneva, the Miura didn't just look good, it went well too, with awesome acceleration, free-revving flexibility and race-inspired roadholding. Build quality aside, how would Lamborghini ever follow it? Well, we didn't have to wait long.

Just as the Miura was more beautiful than most, the Countach, another Gandini design, was one of the most dynamic ever to leap off a designer's note pad. Few cars, not even the other Lamborghinis – the Urraco, Jarama, Silhouette or Jalpa – can bear comparison with the Countach. The body, at the same time curvy and stylish, tough and functional, demands your attention, not least when the gullwing doors rise to their full height, hinged as if by magic on little more than the quarterlight surround. Not even its replacement, the Diablo has such standing, presence and impact. The Lamborghini quad-cam V12 spoke literally for itself, peaking at 455hp in European LP5000s Quatrovalve trim, with 369lb-ft of torque and a top speed of well over 180mph. But figures like these are academic for a car like the Countach. One look says it all.

So is it the ultimate sportscar? Fortunately, only a few lucky owners will know. Which leaves the rest of us to argue, debate and dream for as long as it takes. And there can't be many better pastimes than that.

Above: The Ghibli interior seems to continue the uncluttered look that is a sure giveaway of masterful design, requiring no gimmicks or gadgets to set it above the crowd.

Left and right: Few sportscars possess the beauty of line that is the Maserati Ghibli. Designed by a young Giorgio Giugiaro, then head-designer at Ghia, the Ghibli also packed a twin-cam V8 of 4.7 liters. Only 125 Spyder convertibles were built, compared with over 1100 coupés.

69

SUPER SPORTSCARS

PRANCING HORSES & FLYING SAUCERS

Left: The Ghibli shared its basic chassis and running gear with the Quattroporte sedan and Mexico coupé, though the wheelbase was fixed to suit the Ghibli's precious proportions. At 180 inches long, though, the Ghibli was one of Europe's longest two-seaters. Height was only 46 inches.

SUPER SPORTSCARS

PRANCING HORSES & FLYING SAUCERS

SUPER SPORTSCARS

Previous pages: The De Tomaso Pantera was one of those Italian-American partnerships that never quite won over the sportscar purists. The reason? That Ford V8 nestling in the back of the car behind the ZF five-speed transmission.

Above and right: With a top speed of 130mph (160 in European models unimpeded by emission regulations), and a reasonable price tag, the Pantera became extremely popular when it was introduced in the USA.

74

PRANCING HORSES & FLYING SAUCERS

4. Total Driving Efficiency

TOTAL DRIVING EFFICIENCY

If it's true that a nation's cars reflect their national temperament, then what better example than West Germany. The Italians may be more concerned with the way you do things than what you do, showing their love of the automobile in the sensuous curves of their styling and the highly-strung character of their engines, but the Germans excel in total driving efficiency. Every development is carefully considered, yet innovation is always on the agenda and the closest attention is paid to the finest engineering detail.

It showed from the early days. In the late 1930s it was the BMW 328 that changed the whole idea of what a sportscar should be. BMW had built successful sportscars before, like the 1930 Monte Carlo-winning Dixi roadster and the 1934 315/1, but the 328 was different. At a time when true sportscars were supposed to be brutal, uncompromising and performance based, the BMW was independently sprung with a firm but smooth ride and a small, though highly efficient 2-liter engine. It worked too. In fact, a special bodied version won the Italian Mille Miglia in 1940.

Later BMW sportscars included the 503 Cabriolet, whose performance and handling didn't really live up to its sporty looks, and the stunning 507, which had plenty of go thanks to a 3.2-liter V8, wildly stylish looks and a sky-high price to match. No wonder total production barely topped 250.

With BMW concentrating on sedan development, and it must be said, making a name that has almost become synonymous with fast, upmarket sports sedans, it was many years before the Bayerische Motoren Werke badge appeared on a sportscar again. But when it did, the world couldn't help but take notice. Brainchild of BMW's Motorsport boss, Jochen Neerpasch, the M1 was BMW's first and only mid-engined production car, though in reality the only part that BMW contributed was the engine, a longitudinally-mounted four-valves per cylinder straight six of 3.5-liters. Most of the development work was farmed out to Italians — Lamborghini for the design and Giugiaro's Ital Design for the styling — but the final assembly was carried out at Baur, in West Germany.

Built more as a homologation special than a serious road car, just over 400 were built. Sadly, it barely raced in anger either, though its abilities were impressive. In road trim it was good for 160mph and 0-60mph in 5.5 seconds, but the Group 5 racing version came with no less than 850hp. Fortunately for us all, the demise of the M1 didn't spell the end of the BMW Motorsport division and later M-series cars, like the remarkable M635CSi, M3 and M5, have done more for the marque's prestige reputation than the M1 ever did.

BMW's latest contender in the sports car market, the Z1, is the first product of new BMW division, the specialist research and development complex, known within the company as FIZ. On the face of it, it would be easy to pass off the Z1 as merely a sporty body with gimmicky doors on a 325i floorpan. But closer inspection shows a lot more. To start with there's the composite-fiber sandwich floorpan, exceptionally light at just 33 pounds. Next, the monocoque chassis is galvanized with a zinc filling between the welds, increasing rigidity by a claimed 25 per cent. And finally, the body parts are injection-moulded thermoplastic with all non load-bearing panels easily removable for fast repair. With the doors lowered into the deep rocker sections and the roof folded back beneath its special cover, the Z1 must be the closest the modern sportscar driver can come to reliving the halcyon days of serious wind-in-the-hair motoring.

SUPER SPORTSCARS

TOTAL DRIVING EFFICIENCY

Previous pages: The first in the M Sport range, the BMW M1 was designed by ItalDesign in Turin, Italy.

Left: The M1 body used 10 glass-fiber panels, which were fixed together at the German Baur factory. The finished cars were then taken to BMW Motorsport for tuning and final testing.

Top left: Tough, it was built primarily with racing in mind, the M1 came with electric windows, full stereo system, a comfortable interior and decent luggage space. What a pity that only 400 were built.

Above: A 2.3 liter unit in a BMW M3. Twin cams and Bosch Motronic engine management allow the road driver 200bhp and 177 foot-pounds of torque. Race versions are good for 330bhp.

SUPER SPORTSCARS

Right: The BMW M5 has the understated elegance of an executive saloon, yet all the power of a true sportscar. No less than 315bhp at a roaring 6900rpm and 360 foot-pounds of torque at 4750rpm.

Below: In contrast, the BMW M3 is hardly understated. But it's aimed at a different market. Fortunately, it has all the performance and handling characteristics to match its race-track looks.

80

TOTAL DRIVING EFFICIENCY

Below: The infamous BMW 'Batmobile', the 3.0 CSi in full race trim. Most powerful of the series, the German authorities banned it for public road use when it was first introduced. Top speed was around 137mph.

Above: The BMW Z1 is undoubtedly the most exciting car yet to come with a BMW badge. Note how the doors do not open outwards, but disappear into the rocker panel.

Overleaf: The Z1 looks good with top up or down. Developed by BMW Technik, it boasts a steel monocoque chassis, plastic bodyshell and vertical doors for real open topped motoring.

81

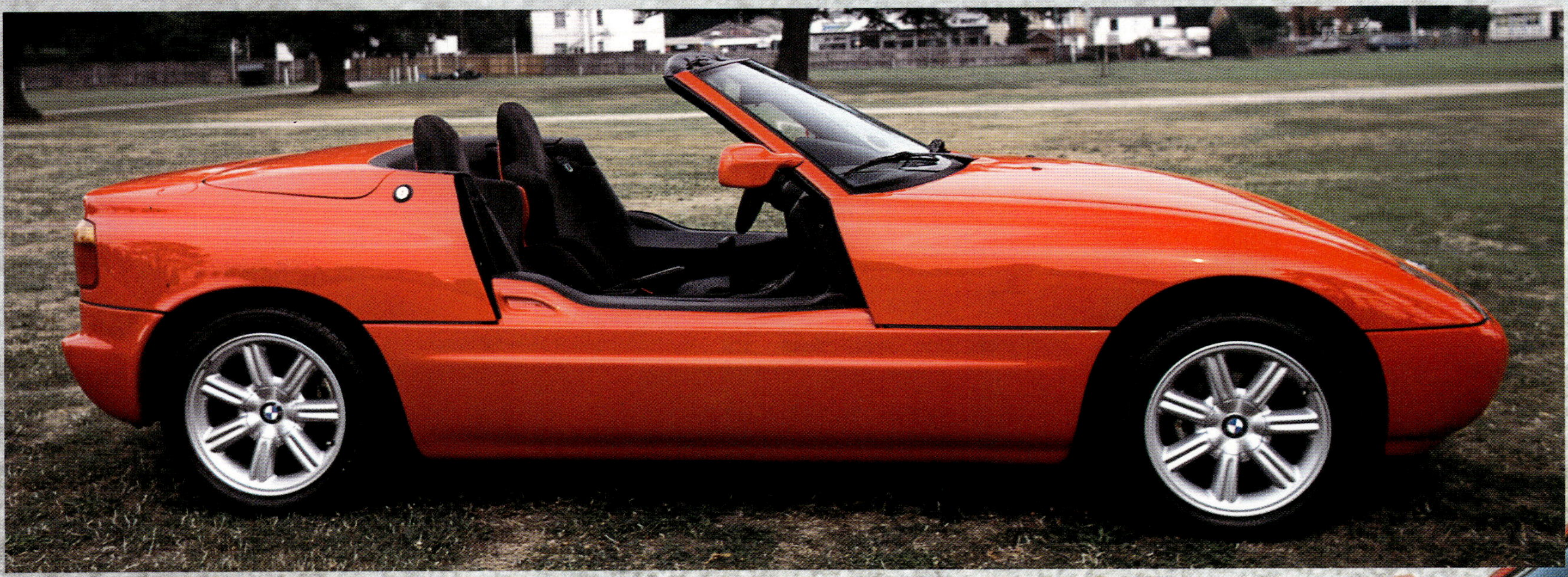

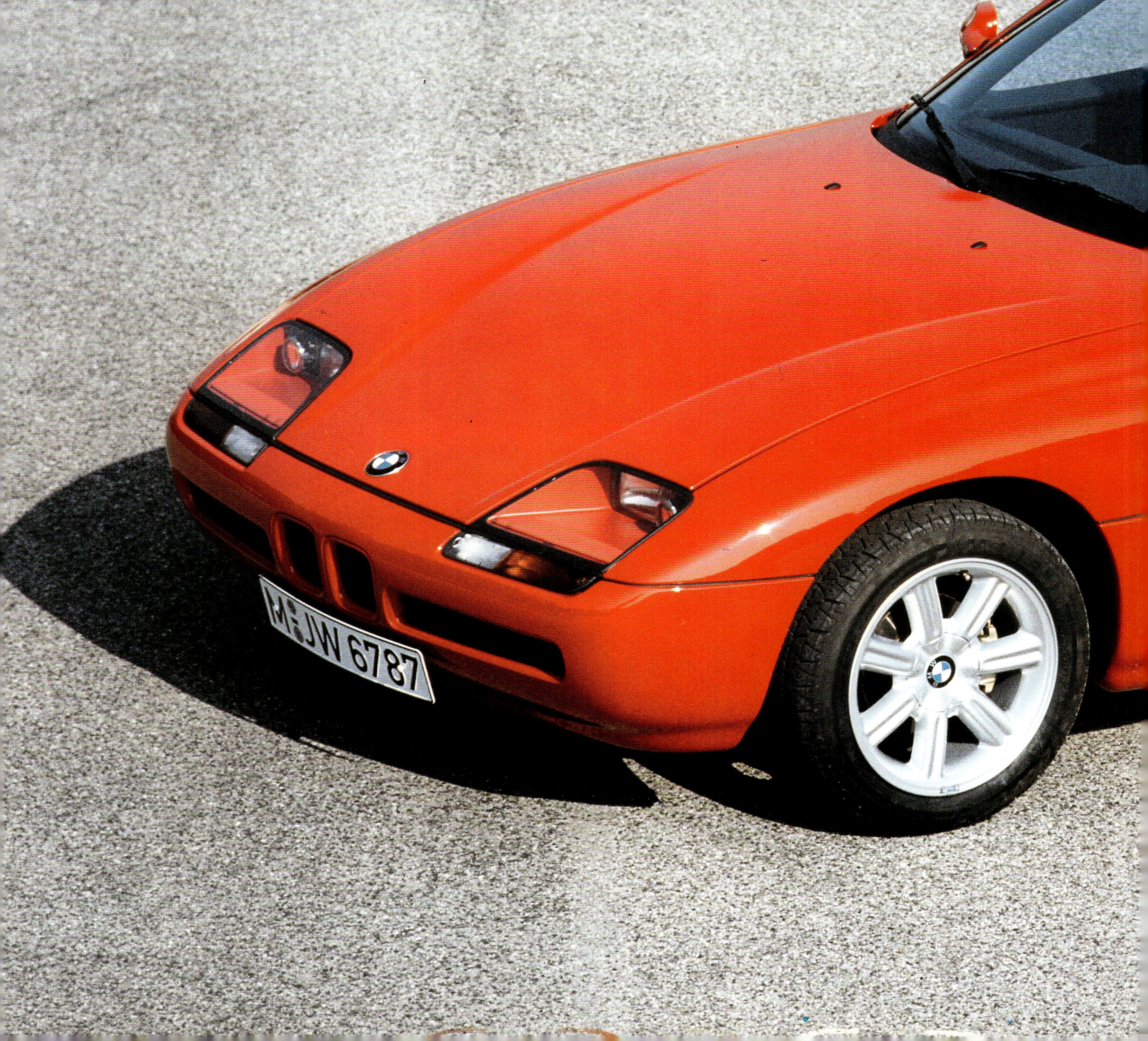
M JW 6787

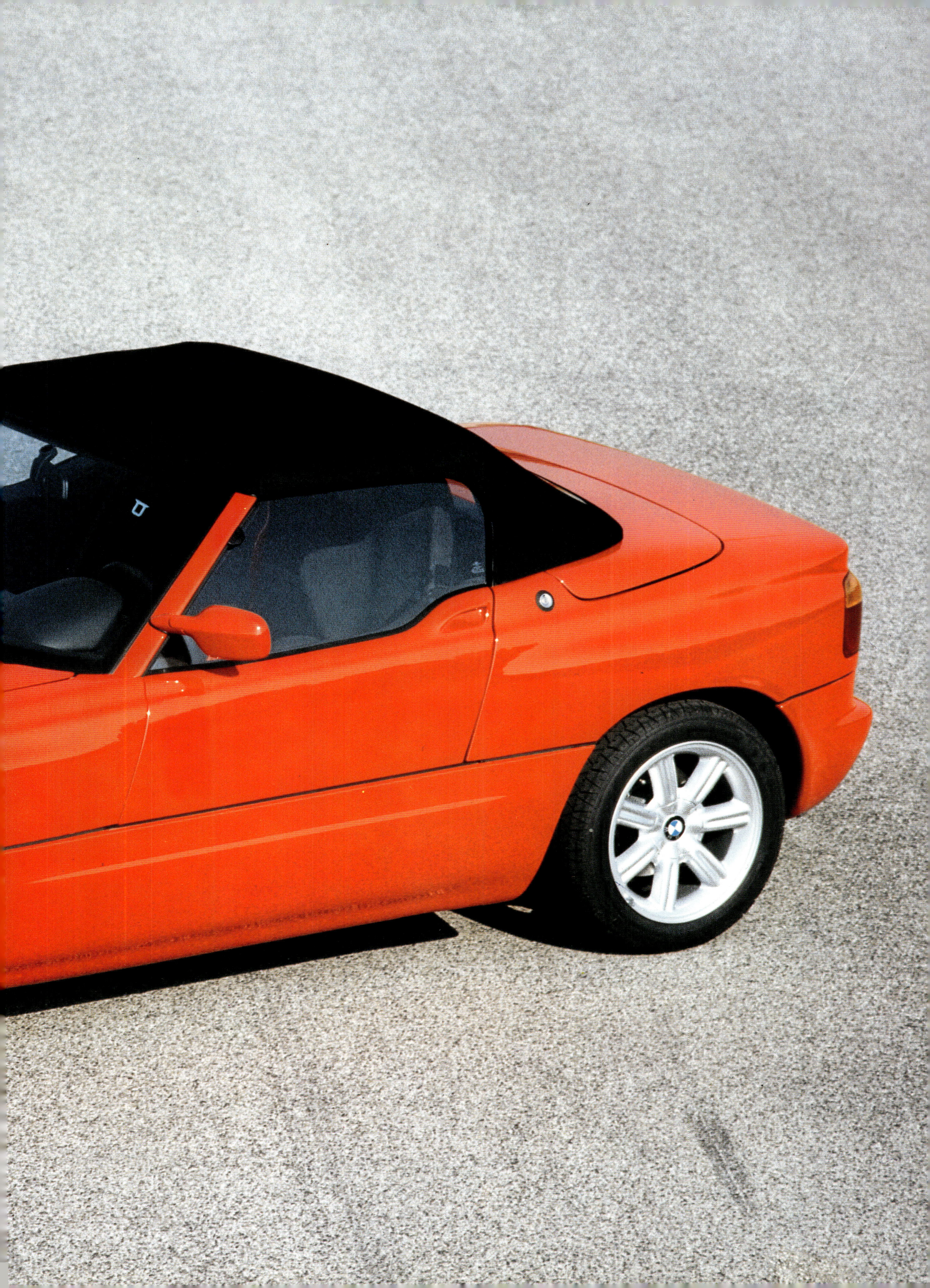

SUPER SPORTSCARS

TOTAL DRIVING EFFICIENCY

Left: Although they are, in fact, a totally independent company, the name Alpina is almost synonymous with BMW sports cars. Running alongside BMW's own M Sport program, the Alpina treatment involves body, engine and suspension work to the owners own specification.

Below left: Based on the new BMW 5 Series, the Alpina B10 looks almost like the stock version. It may have four doors, but don't let that fool you into thinking it won't blow your doors off.

Right: At the luxury end of the sports car market, the Mercedes 350SL started a series that presently continues in the form of the 560SL.

Just as the BMW 328 changed people's opinions about sportscar comfort, so the Mercedes Benz 300SL redefined its role. Launched in 1954, the 300SL raised the limits of 'race and ride' sportscar performance; a car that could win at the track, then allow you to drive home with ease thanks to the engine's incredible flexibility. The swing-axle rear suspension (reminiscent of an early Volkswagen Beetle) did make for entertaining handling, especially in the wet, but the advent of the roadster version in 1957 with its improved rear suspension design, made for higher roll stiffness and less hard cornering heroics.

The 300SL's lightweight multi-tubular space frame chassis used the suspension and running gear from the 300-series sedans, and a 3-liter single overhead cam straight six, with dry sump lubrication and Bosch mechanical fuel injection. The streamlined closed bodywork featured aluminum hood, trunk and gullwing doors, a striking and impressive feature but one which let the water in far more easily than it let its passengers out. The steering wheel tilted to afford slightly easier access over the high rocker panels.

Mercedes Benz have never been renowned for cheap cars, though, and these models in particular fell victim to their high price. In 1956, when a base Corvette would have set you back $2900, the Gullwing was $7300. And by 1960, the 300SL roadster was $11,400. No wonder only 1400 Gullwings and 1858 roadsters were sold. Though at less than half the price, their four-cylinder partner, the 190SL, sold over 25,000 units.

Since 1963, Mercedes roadsters have emphasized luxury rather than performance, with the long line that follows the 230/250/280SL class to 1971, and then the 350/450/380/560SL roadsters right to the present day.

Given that Opel have been owned by General Motors since the 1920s, it is maybe less than surprising that their best known foray into the sportscar market, should be dubbed the 'mini-Corvette'. Like many a sportscar, the Opel GT began life as a one-off show car, revealed at the 1965 Frankfurt Show, but public interest was so great, that the production version appeared just three years later.

Bearing a remarkable, if somewhat stunted resemblance to the '68 Corvette, the GT also featured hidden headlamps and no rear trunk access, but the bodies weren't fiberglass. Built on the humble Opel Kadett GT floorpan with transverse leaf front suspension and a live axle at the rear, it came with two engine choices, a 1.1-liter and the 1.9 which formed the overwhelming majority. At over 100,000 units, the Opel GT was a popular car throughout Europe, and would have sold many more if the Kadett had not been redesigned in '72, leaving the GT without a 'donor' car.

Maybe it was German logic, perhaps it was stubbornness, but the Porsche story begins with a company belief that the best sporting cars were rear-engined. It's a belief they still hold today. Although it may have produced some hairy moments for Porsche drivers, there's no denying that Porsche have taught the world more than a thing or two about performance car technology.

Another Porsche belief, strongly held by Ferry Porsche, Ferdinand's son, was slow but continual model evolution. So from the earliest Volkswagen-derived 356 models, through to the awesome Porsche 959, there is a common thread of Porscheness, a family likeness that defines each and every model. And for many, the water-cooled front-engined Porsches are mere deviations from the masterplan — not real Porsches at all, but 'designer-label' two-seaters, albeit very capable ones.

SUPER SPORTSCARS

TOTAL DRIVING EFFICIENCY

Above left: The Mercedes 380 SLC proved that the two-door coupé versions of the popular SL convertibles could still deliver the goods.

Left: The 450SLC was the US version of the European 350. The extra liter was added to make up for the effects of emission controls.

Above right: The European 350SLC, seen here with optional sunroof and alloy wheels, managed a healthy 230hp from the 3499cc V8.

Right: With a top speed of 160mph, the 1955 Mercedes 300 SL gullwing is one of the most easily recognized cars in the world.

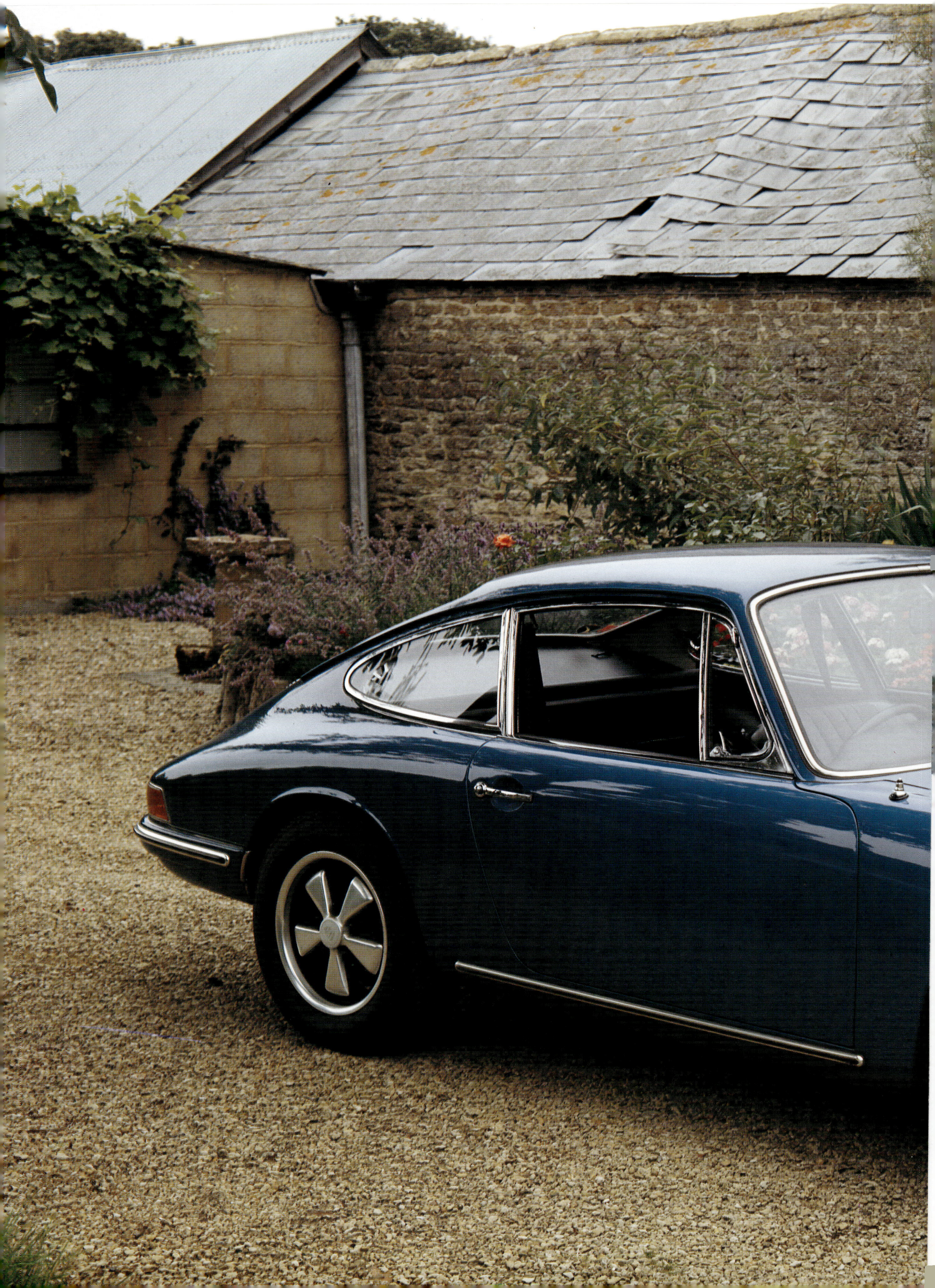

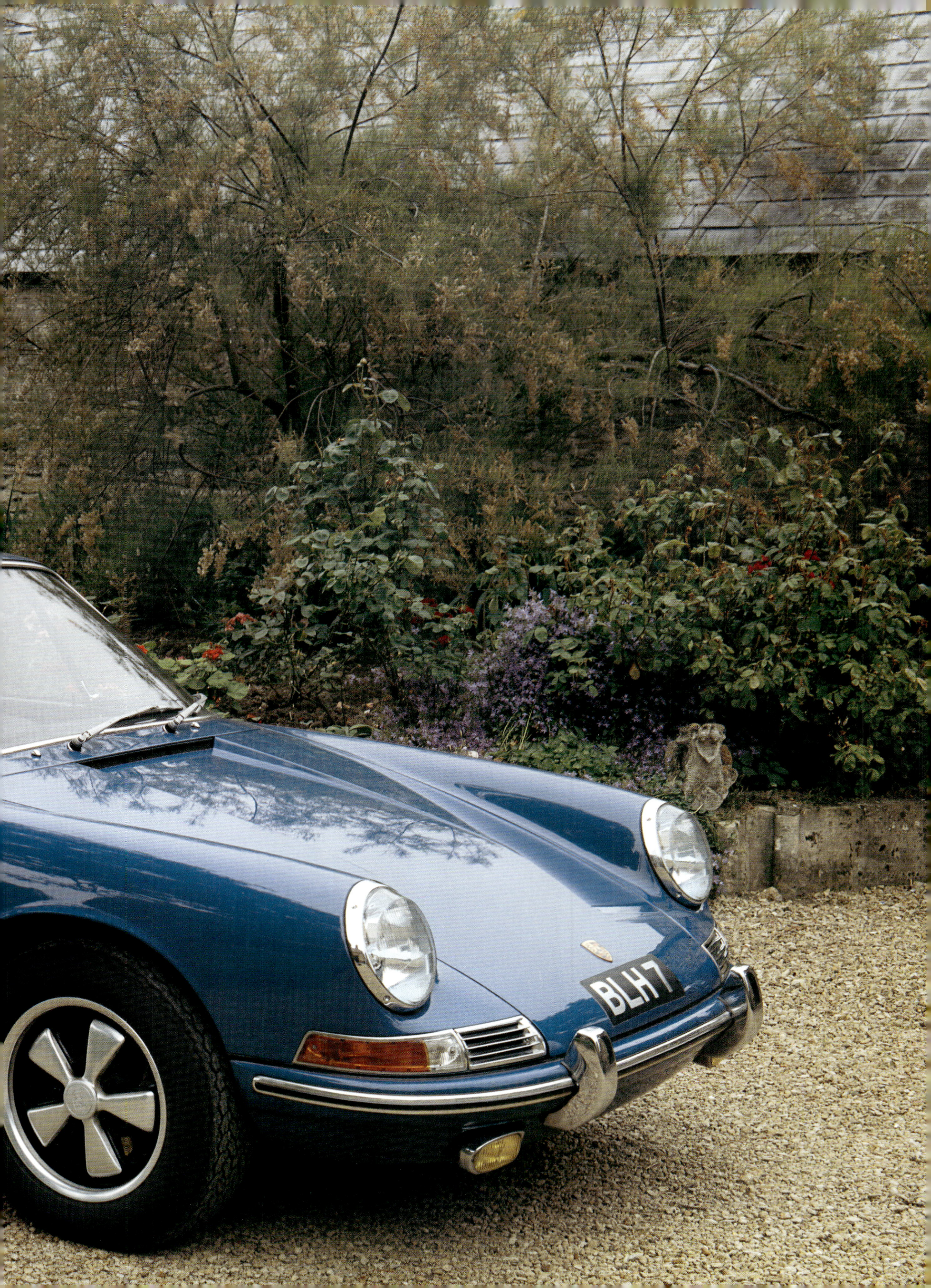
BLH7

SUPER SPORTSCARS

Above: When Porsche revived the 1950s Speedster idea, they began with a 911 Carrera, gave it a slanted, cut-down windshield and added a hump-backed tonneau cover.

Left: At Porsche club meeting is the place to see how the lines of the 911 Porsche have changed over the years. Take your pick.

Right: When the car of your dreams isn't quite what you want, send it to BB who will build you a Turbo Targa like this.

92

TOTAL DRIVING EFFICIENCY

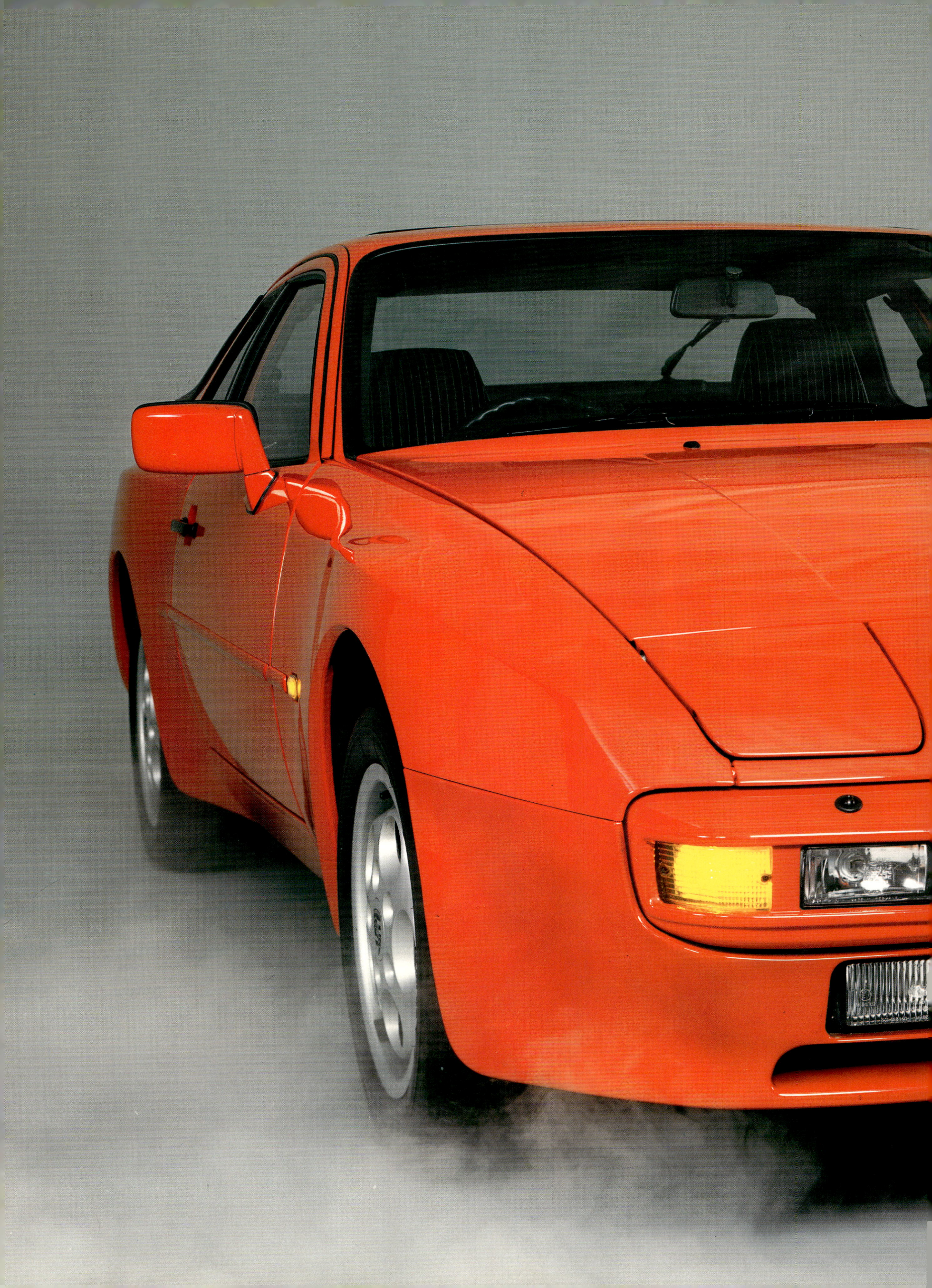

F914 NRX

PORSCHE CARS GREAT BRITAIN LIMITED READING 303666

SUPER SPORTSCARS

Previous pages: It has taken many years for Porsche enthusiasts to come to terms with the fact that a front-engined, water-cooled car would ever carry a Porsche badge at all, let alone that a car like this 944 should be a perfectly respectable sports car in its own right.

Above: One of the most exciting Porsche 924 models was this 924 Turbo. Not to be confused with the 944 Turbo, this model has the giveaway NACA duct on the hood and no extended arches.

Right: Apart from the wheels and the badges, the six-cylinder Porsche 916 was indistinguishable from its four cylinder counterpart, the 914.

96

TOTAL DRIVING EFFICIENCY

Above: Dreams for sale. Only 200 Porsche 959s were built and each became an instant investment. Porsche made a loss on every one, but lucky customers certainly didn't. The 959's twin turbos put out 450hp at 6500rpm, which get to the road via computer controlled four-wheel drive.

Right; Contrasting with the 924 version shown earlier, the 944 Turbo looked beefier all round and packed a good 220bhp at 5800rpm.

97

SUPER SPORTSCARS

Above: The 928, released in March 1977, once again broke new ground for Porsche. With a big watercooled V8 up front, driving a five-speed transaxle at the rear, the car was no disappointment in performance or handling.

Right: First introduced with 240hp, later 928s moved over to fuel injection and ever more power. The latest versions, the Series 4, come with 32 valves and 320hp.

Far right: The exciting 924 Turbo was easily distinguishable by the vents across the nose and two-tone paintwork.

98

TOTAL DRIVING EFFICIENCY

5. Imitation and Innovation

In the halls of sportscar stardom, it's not often that Sweden, Switzerland or even France is mentioned in the same breath as Italy, Germany or Great Britain. Yet history shows that all these countries have indeed produced their fair share of innovative designs. Now the Land of the Rising Sun looks set to teach the world a thing or two about a subject they thought they already knew.

It is said that in every area of economic development, the Japanese have one motto – imitate, then innovate. And this is definitely true of their approach to sportscar design. For a car industry that had designed virtually nothing before the Toyota Crown of 1955, the Japanese can never be accused of slow learning. There were Japanese cars before the Crown, of course, but they were all produced under licensing deals with foreign, usually English or American manufacturers.

The sportscar story starts with the Datsun Fairlady two-seater soft tops of 1959. The 60bhp, 1189cc, S211 Sport was the first of the series, followed by the more powerful S213 and later the more popular Datsun SP310, the 1500, 1600 and 2000 roadsters. A policy of constant improvements and performance hikes, plus a successful SCCA racing program earned Datsun a well-deserved reputation in those early days. Both 1600 and 2000 won SCCA National titles between 1966 and 1971.

The SP310 bore a remarkable resemblance to the British MGB roadster, though it actually pre-dated it. They were very similar in engineering terms too, with twin Hitachi carburetors that looked exactly like British SU's. The cars may not have been sophisticated, nor particularly good looking, but they were excellent value, and they did help pave the way for the famous Datsun Z-series.

The Z-series, beginning with the Datsun 240Z was typical of the Japanese approach. You study every single influential car design in the world, then you build your own. It was also very much a milestone car, as the first Japanese car to sell in huge numbers in the States. But then, considering the value for money if offered, it was hardly surprising. The 2.4-liter in-line six managed 151bhp in US trim, the all-independent suspension offered a comfortable yet sporting ride and the standard interior specification offered a luxury unheard of at the price.

While it is true that subsequent models, the 260Z, 280Z and 280ZX models changed the emphasis from sportscar to luxury sporting two-seater, sales of almost a million for all four cars tell their own story.

Somewhat better looking than its previous California-styled incarnation, the newest Nissan 300ZX with its 3-liter turbo-charged V6, is the latest chapter in the Nissan Z-car story. With up-to-date looks, 280bhp, 0-60mph in just 5.8 seconds and a top speed of 160mph, it's a more than fitting representative of the line.

IMITATION AND INNOVATION

Left: Before they became Nissans, the Datsun 240Z was the car that really brought Japanese sportscars to the rest of the world, starting a series of cars that has totaled over a million units.

Above: The 240Z led to the 260Z. There's not too much to tell them apart from the outside, but on the inside, an increase to 2.6 liters made the difference.

Right: And finally, the 280Z. By now the whole concept of the car was changing to that of a luxury sporting cruiser. The engine was bigger was the sports spirit had all but gone.

SUPER SPORTSCARS

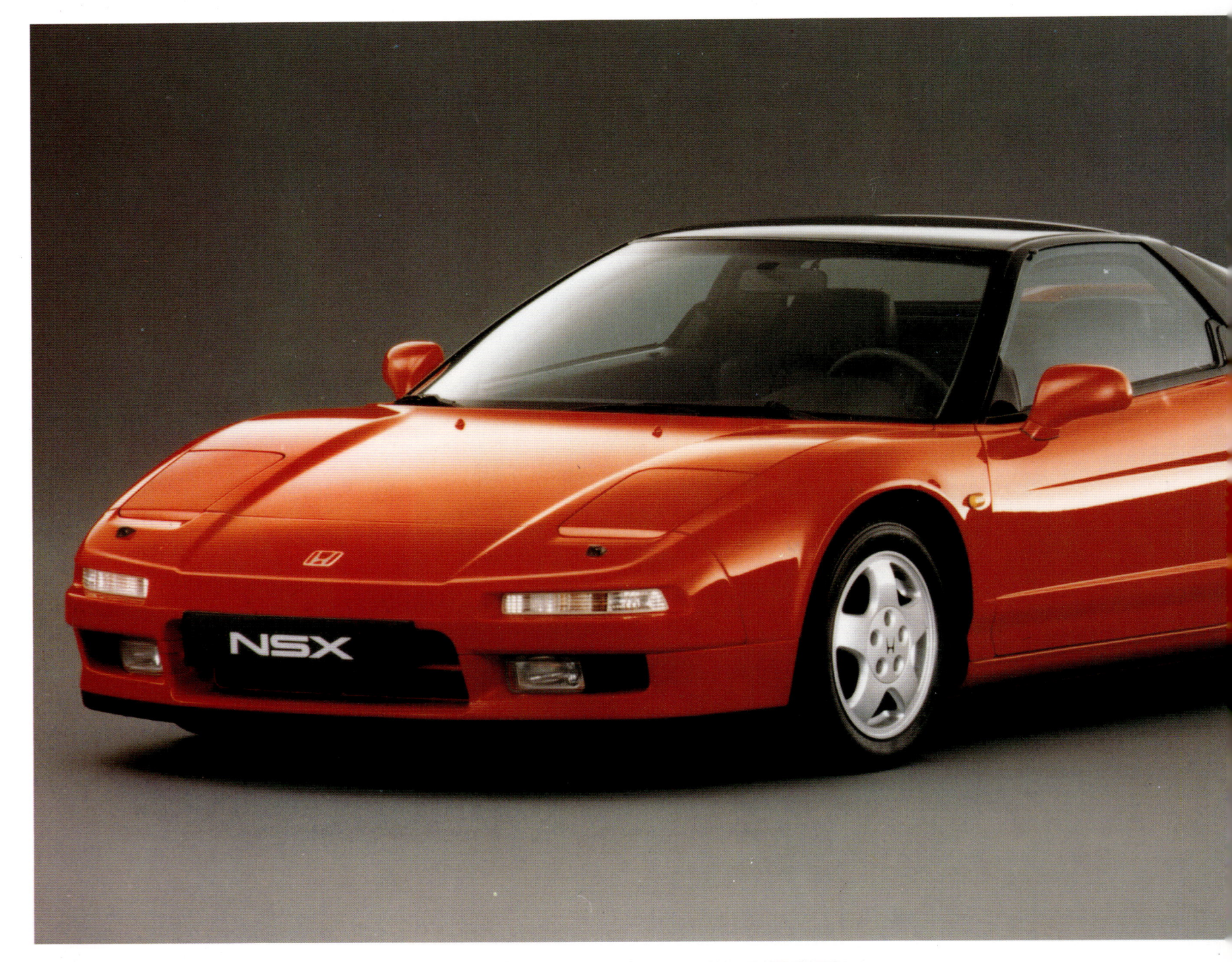

Above and left: The Honda NSX is the latest in a line of Japanese sports cars that look set to teach the motoring establishment a thing or two about advanced automotive technology at an affordable price. A 24-valve 3-liter V6 with variable valve timing and sequential port injection is just the start.

IMITATION AND INNOVATION

Above: Honda's hot hatchback, the CRX 1.6i VT shows what can be done if you watch and wait for a few years before making your move on an unsuspecting market.

Honda's sportscar history begins with the S500, quite an influential little car. Crammed into its tiny two-seater bodywork was an incredible 531cc engine with twin overhead camshafts, four side-draft carburetors, 44bhp and the ability to rev to an unbelievable 8000rpm – indication if any was required, that Honda are just as well known for building motor bikes. The S500 even had chain drive, one to each separate rear axle. The follow up, the S800 moved capacity up to 791cc and 70bhp, but hardly put Honda on the sportscar map.

Given their near domination in the world of racing engines, and the massive inroads made by fellow Japanese manufacturers, it was strange that Honda didn't appear to make more of the sportscar market, confining their performance car aspirations to hot hatchbacks like the CRX. But in 1990, they gave us their answer. The Honda NSX. After the best part of six years in development and more prototypes than many sports cars have seen finished cars, the NSX is Honda's answer to the Ferraris and Porsches of this world.

The specification reads more like that of a racing car. Aluminum monocoque body, chassis and double wishbone suspension, 270PS, 24-valve 3-liter double-overhead cam V6 engine with Honda's V-TEC (variable valve timing), VVIS (variable volume induction) and sequential port fuel injection (PGM-FI), direct ignition with a separate coil for each cylinder, titanium conrods, switchable traction control, antilock brakes, 0-60 in under 6 seconds and a top speed over 165mph says all you need to know about its performance and roadholding capabilities. What it doesn't tell you, however, is that this car is as easy to drive as a Honda Civic.

Instead of copying what had gone before, Toyota went it alone for their first sportscar. And you could say it looked it. You could not deny that the Sports 800 was innovative, though. Lightweight construction, a twin-cylinder, air-cooled 790cc engine, with hemi heads and hydraulic lifters, and torsion bar suspension were all part of the make up, but the car was never exported so many still regard their next creation, the curvy 2000 GT as their first real attempt.

Bearing a close resemblance to the Jaguar XKE, the 2000 GT even came with an in-line six-cylinder engine with twin overhead cams and three Mikuni-Solex carburetors. Although it was a serious sportscar in every respect, from its fully independent suspension to its magnesium alloy wheels, the 2000 GT was more of a PR exercise for Toyota than a serious attempt at the market. For a start the price was very steep, and secondly, they were only available in right-hand drive as if for home consumption alone.

Yet to increase world awareness of the marque, Toyota contracted Caroll Shelby to campaign the car in SCCA C production class, and even got it a part in the Bond movie *You Only Live Twice* (though they did cut the roof off). By the end of production in 1970, Toyota had only shifted 337 units.

103

SUPER SPORTSCARS

Although the Celica and Supra would make hefty inroads into the performance market, we had to wait 15 years for the next true sportscar from Toyota. But the MR2 was definitely worth the wait. Although it was virtually a corporate kit car, with transverse engine, transaxle and suspension from the Corolla, the MR2 had a character all of its own, a personality retained in the newly restyled 2-liter 1990 version, which in GT 16-valve trim boasts 158bhp.

In a world where every manufacturer offers basically the same package wrapped up in a different parcel, it is rare to come across something truly different. And even rarer to find a company prepared to back it to the hilt. The Wankel rotary engine is definitely something different and Toyo Kogyo Co Ltd, or Mazda as their line of cars is known, is that company.

It's incredible that Mazda produced anything at all after the war, given that their factory was at Hiroshima, yet they were producing vehicles only months after the atomic bomb had killed over 400 of their employees. Their first sportscar, the Cosmo 110S, debuted at the Tokyo Motor Show in 1964.

Another right-hand drive only car, the 110S may not have proved a runaway success, but it did prove the viability of the Wankel engine. By 1973, Mazda had sold half a million vehicles with rotary engines, including, of course, the RX-7 sportscar.

The RX-7 offered sleek lines, good handling and smooth rotary power. Apart from the engine, it was quite a simple machine, with a front-engine rear-wheel drive layout, MacPherson struts at the front and a solid rear axle. The second generation RX-7 of 1986 took things further with Porsche-like styling, independent rear suspension, and even an intercooled, turbo-charged and injected engine. Most recently there is even a cabriolet version, which with its little sister, the normally-engined MX5, announces loud and clear that Mazda are going to stay in the sportscar business for some time to come.

IMITATION AND INNOVATION

Left: Popularizing the Wankel engine, the Mazda RX-7 offered good looks and plenty of go. Apart from its advanced engine, the car's engineering was quite simple, with rear-wheel drive and MacPherson struts front suspension.

Above: Mazda's latest move on the sportscar market opened more than a few eyes, when it resurrected the small open topped roadster in the form of the MX-5. This example wears an optional hardtop.

Right: The MX-5's interior is compact, simple and functional.

105

SUPER SPORTSCARS

Above: The Mitsubishi 3000GT VR-4, seen here at the NEC, Motor Show, England, is another new wave Japanese supercar. It's sold in the USA as the Dodge Stealth R/T Turbo and has been described as 'one of the most capable cars on the planet'.

Right: At the same venue, the Mitsubishi HSR II gave us a taste of what's to come in future Japanese sports cars.

Japan's latest entrants to the lucrative sportscar club are Mitsubishi (meaning three diamonds, hence their logo), but their debut, the Starion displays no lack of experience. In its latest ES1-R configuration, the car features eight-way adjustable shocks, four wheel discs, antilock rear brakes, 16-inch wheels, and a 2.6-liter four-cylinder engine that is injected, intercooled, turbo-charged and uses the same counterbalance system as the Porsche 944.

And as if that wasn't enough, the latest Mitsubishi, a joint venture with Dodge of America, pushes back the frontiers of sportscar technology to even greater limits. The Mitsubishi 3000GT VR-4, or Dodge Stealth R/T Turbo (they are even built at the same Japanese factory) has been described as 'one of the most capable cars on the planet' by one magazine. But then with a specification that includes every trick in the book, it jolly well should be.

The twin-turbo 3-liter V6, mounted transversely in the front of the car, uses aluminum alloy heads with two cams per bank. The power output is 300bhp at 6000rpm; the torque, an incredible 307lb-ft at just 2500rpm. The four-wheel drive system uses a variable torque split with viscous coupling. First gear will take you to 45mph, second to 80mph and third well past 120, while the antilock brakes will bring you to a swift, safe halt, whatever the conditions.

From late starter to world beater in just 30 years, there is no denying that Japan holds the key to the future of driveable, affordable, supercars. And maybe now that even the mighty Dodge have caught on to the fact, the rest of the world will realize that we won't beat 'em, so we may as well join 'em.

IMITATION AND INNOVATION

107

SUPER SPORTSCARS

Above: When Volvo first announced the P1800, it was so unusual for this builder of ordinary cars, that it caused quite a sensation. Although the company are Swedish, the cars were assembled in Britain by Jensen.

Right: Roger Moore did much to popularize the Volvo P1800, as Simon Templar in TV's *The Saint*, though with yearly produciton of around 5000 units, it was hardly a massive success.

Far right: The P1800 interior possessed that classic '60s look, with leather trim and plenty of chrome.

IMITATION AND INNOVATION

For a part of the world that has produced some of the greatest rally drivers we have ever known, Scandinavia's sportscar output has been remarkably low. Volvo's nearest, the 1800 series, can only be described as sports coupés and Saab's claim to fame, the Sonnett, hardly rates a mention.

Built by the Pressed Steel Company in Britain and assembled at Jensen because Volvo had no spare capacity to build them themselves, the P1800's running gear originally came from the Volvo Amazon sedan. The name was changed to 1800S when production moved back to Sweden in 1964, 1800E when fuel injection was added and 1800ES when it became a sports Wagon in 1971. To say that Volvo never built a true sportscar, however, would be to do them an injustice, as they did build the P1900, a fiberglass convertible, in 1956. Only 67 ever made it out of the factory gates. Saab experimented with a two-seat roadster in the mid-'50s too, but again very few were built. Its replacement, the Sonnett II didn't appear until 1966.

Unlike its forerunner, the Sonnett II was a diminutive coupé, built on a Saab 96 sedan floorpan. The styling didn't exactly take your breath away, maybe because it was designed by an aircraft company and built by a railway works. And its 841cc two-stroke engine didn't exactly set the world alight either, though it did gain a Ford V4 in 1968, the version that was marketed in the States.

The Sonnett III of 1970-74 was still nothing to write home about in the styling department, despite Italian design by Sergio Coggiola. It had moved to 1.7 liters by now, but the heavier body with its big impact bumpers, made it just as sluggish. Saab never got involved in the sportscar world again, preferring to put their name on the type of luxury sports sedan characterized by the latest, the 9000 2.3 Turbo TCS, which squeezes 200bhp and an incredible 243lb-ft of torque out of its four Garrett T25 turbo-charged cylinders.

Moving south a thousand miles or so, Switzerland isn't exactly the first name that springs to mind when you think of sportscars, either. Yet Peter Monteverdi, a BMW dealer and former racing driver, built quite a name for his luxury sports cars in the late '60s and early '70s. Assembled by his own workshop staff in between BMW services, most of his cars used bought-in components, hung on one of his own heavy tube chassis. Power usually came from giant Chrysler V8s, either the 440ci or 426ci Hemi units. The names of the car came from the power outputs – the 375S came with 375hp, the later 400SS had 400hp – and bodywork was usually by Fissore of Turin to designs by Frua.

Monteverdi's other models included the Hai (or shark), a mid-engined coupé with Hemi power, built to compete with the Lamborghini Muira, the 375/4, a luxury four-door, and the Berlinetta, a 375S two-seater, again with the Hemi engine putting out 450bhp. But as the recession in the early '70s began to bite, demand dried to a trickle and Monteverdi concentrated on mild customizing treatments for an assortment of vehicles. And of course, servicing BMWs.

After prewar names like Bugatti, Delage, Hispano-Suiza and Hotchkiss, the modern day French contribution to the sportscar world seems very little, especially compared with the way the Italians took hold of the market. The big names either faded competely, taken over or closed down, while the others, like Peugeot, the longest running car company of them all, forsook sportscars in later years for the high volume world of the family sedan. Peugeot's only concession to wind-in-the-hair motoring were cabriolet versions of two sedans, the 304 of 1975 with its four-cylinder 1288cc engine and the 504 with body by PininFarina and the new jointly developed Renault/Peugeot/Volvo V6.

In postwar times it was left to Jean Daninos to uphold the French reputation for exclusive coachbuilt luxury cars. His company, Facel, built some beautiful examples, though many, like the Vega, FVS and HK500, were more in the way of big cruisers than sports cars. The only convertible was the Facellia.

Launched in 1959, the Facellia was a lot smaller than previous Facels. At first it came with a twin-cam four from Weslake in England, but unreliability problems got the cars such a bad name that changes to Volvo, and then Austin Healey 3000 engines couldn't stop the slide into receivership and by 1963 it was almost all over. The Facel II, a sporty two-seater coupé with a 383ci Chrysler engine, lasted just one year longer, which was a great pity for such an attractive car.

If France lacked anything in postwar coachbuilding skills, they certainly didn't lack when it came to motor racing. Matra, who dominated so many areas of motor sport for ten years, eventually winning the World Championship in 1969 with Jackie Stewart, are a prime case in point.

When Matra (Mechanique-Aviation-Traction), one of France's leading aeronautical and missile engineering companies, took over Bonnet, an ailing French sports car company, the Bonnet Djet became the Matra Djet. But for many years their racing activities overshadowed any road car projects, and their first attempt, the Matra 530 failed because Ford, who supplied the V4 engines, refused to handle the marketing.

109

SUPER SPORTSCARS

Lessons learnt, they went to Chrysler of France with their next project and the Simca-engined, Matra-Simca Bagheera was born. Introduced in 1973, this road car sported an attractive low-slung, glass-fiber body with three front seats, side by side. Powered by the Simca 1300cc engine, it was surprisingly nippy too.

While Matra joined hands with Chrysler, Alpine ended up with Renault. And like Matra, Alpine made their name on the race track rather than the road. Operating from a small garage in Dieppe on the northern coast of France, Jean Redele, the company's founder, started by winning the 750cc class in the Mille Miglia for three years running in a hopped up Renault 4CV and continued to forge quite a reputation.

It was only when Matra beat them to a big sponsorship deal from the French government to win Formula 1 for France, that Alpine withdrew from racing in 1969 and went into rallying instead, using the A110 with its Renault R16 engine. In 1600S form this gave 138bhp at 6000rpm and prove a very agile contender on the rallies of Europe as many an outright win, like their 1, 2, 3, clean sweep at Monte Carlo in 1971 was to prove.

The A110's long-awaited follow-up, the A310 was Alpine's first new car for eight years. Unlike previous cars, it was aimed primarily at the road market. Far larger, more spacious and luxurious than the A110, the A310 was powered by another four-cylinder R16 engine at first, though this was later replaced by a V6. By now, Alpine was totally in Renault's hands, yet they held off with a new model, the Alpine-Renault the GTA until 1985.

Larger still, the GTA packs a more aerodynamic shape (a Cd of just 0.28), a bonded steel/fiberglass monocoque and a longitudinally-mounted 200bhp, 2458cc turbo-charged engine from the top-of-the-range Renault 25 sedan. With its all-independent suspension, five-speed transmission and four-wheel discs, it's as fast as it looks too, peaking at 155mph. The only sad thing is that it's not available in the USA.

Last, but not least, comes an oddity. It's not every day you hear of a four-door sportscar, but the French built a stunning one. Looking for all the world like a latter day Lamborghini, the Monique (named after his wife) was the brainchild of one Jean Tastevin, with design chores in the hands of British race car tuner Chris Lawrence. And what a car it was — semi-space frame chassis, rocker arm front suspension, DeDion rear axle and a Chrysler V8. They say it takes all sorts to make a world, but a sportscar with four doors? I wonder what reasons they gave for its failure?

Below: One of the few latter day French sports cars, this Renault Alpine was prepared for the 1972 Acropolis rally in Greece, with much wider wheels and extended arches.

Right: Contrast the early Alpine with this late model GTA. With its low co-efficient of drag, and healthy Renault V6 engine, it's good for 155mph.

IMITATION AND INNOVATION

Index

AC Cobra 28, *37, 38*
Acropolis rally, Greece *110*
Alfa Romeo 53, *64*
Allard, Sydney 26, 27
Arnold, S H "Wacky" 10
  Arnold-Bristol 10
Aston Martin *27, 28, 30,* 38
Audi 89
Austin-Healey 6, 27, 28, 109

Baracca, Franco 56
Barracuda 9
Baur, West Germany *79*
Bentley 6
Bertone 53, *64,* 69
BMW 77, *79, 80, 81, 85, 85,* 109
  Technik *81*
Bond, James 45
Bonneville Salt Flats *10*
Bricklin, Malcolm 10
Brooklands *38*
Brown, David *27,* 38
Bugatti 60, 109

Cadillac 6, 10, 27
Car and Driver magazine 18
Caterham Cars 32
Challenger 9
Chapman, Colin 26, 30, *43*
Charger 9
Chevrolet 11, 12, *14,* 18
  Corvette *6.* 9, 11, 12, 18, *18, 23, 24, 25,* 30, 32
Chrysler 27, 30, 109, 110
Citroën 64
Cobra 9, 12, 28, 30
Coggiola, Sergio 109
Cole, Edward 12, 14
Colombo, Gioacchino 56
Costin, Frank 26
Coventry Climax 32
Crosley Junior, Powel 10

Daimler *32*
Daninos, Jean 109
Darrin, Howard 'Dutch' 10
Datsun 100, *101*
Daytona Beach 14, *18*
Delage 109
De Lorean, John 10, *14*
De Tomaso 65, *73, 75*
De Tomaso, Alejandro 65
Dodge 106, *106*
Duntov, Zora Arkus 12, 14

Earl, Harley 12, 14

Facel 109
Ferrari 6, *6,* 33, 53, *53,* 56, 57, *57, 57, 59* 60, 64
  Scuderia 56
Ferrari, Enzo 53, 56, 57, *57*
Fiat 53, 60, *67*
Ford 9, 10, *10,* 12, *13,* 27, 30, 38, *41*
Frankfurt Motor Show 85, 88

Gable, Clark 27
Gandini, Marcello *63,* 69
Gauntlett, Victor 38
Geneva Show 60, 64, *67,* 89
Ghia 53, 65, *69*
Giugiaro, Giorgio 10, 53, *64, 69*
GM (General Motors) 10, 11, 12, 18, 33, *42*

Halfet, Keith *50*
Haussauer, Paul 32
Healey, Donald 26, 28, *35*
Hiroshima 104
Hispano-Suiza 109
Honda *102,* 103, *103*
Hotchkiss 109

ItalDesign 53, 64, 77, *79*

Jaguar 6, 33, 35, 37, 38, *48, 50*
Jensen 28, 30, *108*
  Alan 27
  Richard 27
Jensen-Healey 28, *35*

Kaiser-Darrin 10
Kimber, Cecil 26, 33
King Midget 10
Kurtis, Frank 10

Lamborghini *61, 63,* 65, 69, 77, 109
Lamborghini, Ferruccio 65
Lancia 53, *67*
Lancia, Vincenzo 60
Lawrence, Chris 110
Lawson, Geoff *50*
Le Mans 30, *41*
Lotus *6, 25,* 26, 30, 32, 33, *42, 43, 44, 45*
Lyons, William 26, 33

Maranello 56
Marcos 26, 27, *32*
Marsh, Jem 26
Maserati 56, 60, 64, *69,* 71
  Officina Alfieri Maserati 60
Matra 109
Mazda 104, *105*

Mercedes Benz 85, *85,* 87
MG (Morris Garages) 33, *46*
Mille Miglia 77, 110
Mini Cooper 6
Mitchell, Bill 12, 18
Mitsubishi 106, *106*
Monte Carlo rally 60, *67,* 77
Monteverdi, Peter 109
Moore, Roger *108*
Morgan *6,* 26, *35*

NEC Motor Show, England *106*
Neerpasch, Jochen 77
Nissan 100, *101*

Opel 85
OSCA 60

Pebble Beach 27
Peugeot 109
Piech, Ferdinand 88
Pininfarina 53, 60, 64
Plymouth Superbird 9
Pontiac *9*
Porsche *6,* 88, 89, *89, 92, 96, 97, 98*
  Ferdinand 'Butzi' 88
  Ferdinand, Dr 85, 88
  Ferry 85, 88

Qvale, Kjell 27

Redele, Jean 110
Renault 11, *14,* 109, 110, *110*
Reutter Carrosserie 88
Roadrunner 9
Rootes Group 30

Saab 109
Saint, The 108
Sayer, Malcolm 37
Sebring 12 Hours 14
Shelby, Carroll 28, 30, *37, 41,* 103
Shelby Cobra 28, 30

Tastevin, Jean 110
Thompson, Mickey *10*
Tjaarda, Tom 65, *73*
Tokyo Motor Show 104
Tomala, Hans 88
Touring, Milan 64
Towns, William 38
Toyo Kogyo Co Ltd 104
Toyota 110, 103, 104
Triumph *32,* 33, *34*
TVR 30, *46*

Vector *14, 17*

Vignale, Turin 64
Volkswagen 88, 89
Volvo *108,* 109

Watkins Glen 27
Wiegart, Gerald *14, 17*
Wilkinson, Trevor 26

ACKNOWLEDGMENTS
The publisher would like to thank the following for their help in the preparation of this book: Adrian Hodgkins the designer, Helen Dawson for the index, Veronica Price for production. We are also grateful to the following individuals and agencies for use of the pictures on the pages noted below:

Autocar: pages 28, 97 (below).
National Motor Museum, Beaulieu: pages 34 (top), 44-5, 58 (below), 94-5, 97 (top).
BMW: pages 78 (below), 81 (below), 82-3, 84 (both).
Brompton Picture Library: pages 6-7, 8, 9, 11 (both), 12, 13, 15, 16, 17, 18 (top), 19(both), 22-23, 25 (both), 26-7, 36, 64-5 76-7, 93.
Neill Bruce: pages 1, 2-3, 14 (both), 29 (both), 30, 34 (below), 35 (both), 37, 39, 42, 43, 48 (below), 49, 50 (both), 51 (both), 52, 56, 57, 58 (top), 62 (below), 64 (top), 65 (top), 66 (top pair), 67 (top), 68, 69 (both), 70-1, 78 (top), 85, 86 (both), 87 (both), 90-1, 100, 101, 104, 105 (both), 106, 107, 111.
Neill Bruce/Peter Roberts Collection: pages 102 (both), 103.
General Motors: pages 4-5
Norman Hodson: pages 79, 80 (both).
Link House Magazine: page 66-7.
Marcos Cars: page 33
Andrew Morland: pages 44, 48 (top), 72-3, 74, 75 (both), 92 (top), 96 (below).
Don Morley: pages 18 (below), 19 (top).
Quadrant: pages 31, 32, 109, 110
Porsche: pages 92, 96 (top), 98 (below).
Marty Schorr: page 10
Richard Spiegelmann: page 24 (both).
TPS/CCI: page 62
TRH: pages 54-5, 98 (top).
TVR Engineering Ltd: pages 46 (both), 47 (top)
Volvo: page 108 (both).
Stuart Windsor: pages 81 (top), 82 (top).
Nicky Wright: pages 13 (both), 20-21, 47 (below), 88, 99

112

SUPER SPORTSCARS